Translation and Social Media Communication in the Age of the Pandemic

This collection of essays represents the first of its kind in exploring the conjunction of translation and social media communication, with a focus on how these practices intersect and transform each other against the backdrop of the cascading COVID-19 crisis. The contributions in the book offer empirical case studies as well as personal reflections on the topic, illuminating a broad range of themes such as knowledge translation, crisis communications, language policies, cyberpolitics and digital platformization. Together they demonstrate the vital role of translation in the trust-based construction of global public health discourses, while accounting for the new medialities that are reshaping the conception, experience and critique of translation in response to the cultural, political and ecological challenges in a post-pandemic world.

Written by leading scholars in translation studies, media studies and literary studies, this volume sets to open up new conversations among these fields in relation to the global pandemic and its aftermath.

Tong King Lee is Associate Professor of Translation at the University of Hong Kong.

Dingkun Wang is Assistant Professor of Translation at the University of Hong Kong.

Routledge Focus on Translation and Interpreting Studies

Translation and Social Media Communication in the Age of the Pandemic
Edited by Tong King Lee and Dingkun Wang

For more information about this series, please visit: https://www.routledge.com/Routledge-Focus-on-Translation-and-Interpreting-Studies/book-series/RFTIS

Translation and Social Media Communication in the Age of the Pandemic

Edited by
Tong King Lee and
Dingkun Wang

Routledge
Taylor & Francis Group
NEW YORK AND LONDON

First published 2022
by Routledge
605 Third Avenue, New York, NY 10158

and by Routledge
4 Park Square, Milton Park, Abingdon, Oxon, OX14 4RN

Routledge is an imprint of the Taylor & Francis Group, an informa business

Library of Congress Cataloguing-in-Publication Data
A catalog record for this title has been requested

ISBN: 978-1-032-02558-2 (hbk)
ISBN: 978-1-032-02560-5 (pbk)
ISBN: 978-1-003-18390-7 (ebk)

DOI: 10.4324/9781003183907

Typeset in Times New Roman
by MPS Limited, Dehradun

Contents

Figures

Contributors

Donya Alinejad is Assistant Professor of Media and Cultural Studies at Utrecht University.

Susan Bassnett is Professor of Comparative Literature at the University of Glasgow.

Patrick Cadwell is Assistant Professor of Translation Studies at Dublin City University.

Renée Desjardins is Associate Professor in the School of Translation at the Université de Saint-Boniface.

Bei Hu is Assistant Professor in the Department of Chinese Studies at the National University of Singapore.

Tong King Lee is Associate Professor of Translation at the University of Hong Kong.

Tetyana Lokot is Associate Professor in Digital Media and Society at Dublin City University.

Sharon O'Brien is Professor of Translation Studies at Dublin City University.

Anthony Pym is Professor of Translation Studies at the University of Melbourne.

Ilan Stavans is Lewis-Sebring Professor of Humanities and Latin American and Latino Culture at Amherst College.

José van Dijck is Distinguished University Professor of Media and Digital Society at Utrecht University.

Mª Carmen África Vidal Claramonte is Professor of Translation at the University of Salamanca.

Dingkun Wang is Assistant Professor of Translation at the University of Hong Kong.

Acknowledgements

This publication is supported by the Louis Cha Fund (East-West Studies), administered by the Faculty of Arts, University of Hong Kong.

Introduction

Translation in the time of #COVID-19

Tong King Lee and Dingkun Wang

The onslaught of COVID-19 has no doubt brought about the worst of times in recent history. Regimes of border controls, lockdown, quarantine, safe distancing and viral testing, instituted by states around the world in fulfilment of public health imperatives, continue to impinge on us at the time of this writing. These regimes, as Giorgio Agamben provokes, are the instantiation of an emergent pretext (after terrorism) invented to strengthen state surveillance over the individual body. In the wake of a life-threatening viral situation, we find ourselves in an impelling bind, 'a perverse vicious circle' where 'the limitation of freedom imposed by governments is accepted in the name of a desire for security that was induced by those same governments that are now intervening to satisfy it' (Agamben 2020: n.p.).

It is against this backdrop that one aspect of our social life can perhaps be said to be experiencing, as it were, the best of times—social media communication. The virtual and ever-proliferating networks of social media represent the obverse of our physical world in these pandemic times, as characterized by impeded travel and restricted mobilities. Prolonged isolation at homes or in hotels and altered proxemics arising from distancing measures have intensified feelings of estrangement. This has prompted individuals to volume up on social media communications, as if in compensation for their loss in pre-COVID interactivities. The upshot of this is that we are encountering not just an epidemic; as Tedros Adhanom Ghebreyesus, Director-General of the World Health Organization tells us, we are also faced with an *infodemic*, marked by the spread of mis- and dis-information in cyberspaces where scientific knowledge concerning life and death is sometimes distorted or misinterpreted.[1]

This is not to say that social media communications are entirely bottom-up; on the contrary, governments, official institutions, NGOs, commercial agents, too, tap into the affordances of social media for

DOI: 10.4324/9781003183907-1

their own various purposes during the pandemic. Social media, then, represent a complex site of contestation among different players, who bring their communication practices, professional agendas, and ideological persuasions to converge on apparently egalitarian, rhizomatic platforms. The situation is further complicated by the fact that pandemic-related communications are asymmetrically exchanged among any number of languages worldwide, which makes translation a pertinent issue.

This collection of essays locates itself at the conjunction of translation and social media communication, with an eye towards how the two lines of inquiry intersect with and feed into each other against the backdrop of the cascading crisis. To this end the contributions in this volume offer different angles on the relationship between translation and social media communication, prompting us to think about the implications of communication-as-translation and translation-as-communication during pandemic times for translation studies and the humanities more generally.

Memes and knowledge translation: Communication as translation

We ask, first of all, how translation adds value to the way we think about communication in social media. One of the most prominent vehicles of contemporary social media discourse are memes. In their dialogic chapter, **África Vidal Claramonte** and **Ilan Stavans**[2] speak of memes as 'internet translations', where memes are defined as semiotic units that 'reconfigure, rewrite, and translate contemporary issues based on an original (an image, a film, a song, a text) which the target audience recognizes'. The language of memes, as the authors tell us, is 'an infinite translation'. COVID-19 has unsurprisingly given rise to a proliferation of creative memes in social media—from humorous and entertaining GIF images to factious and hate-mongering ones—as if in compensation for the increased physical isolation brought upon by pandemic lockdowns.

It seems that the more socially distanced we are from one another, the greater the imperative to translate our ideas and thoughts virtually through these 'astonishingly creative forms of communication', which transport us from our 'Robinson Crusoe Island into a marketplace of meaning'. But this 'marketplace of meaning' is not necessarily idyllic and innocent. In a memorable phrasing, **Vidal** and **Stavans** describe pandemic memes as 'semiotic hand-grenades', reminding us that—not unlike translation—they can cut both ways. More specifically, they can be multimodal resources for the sharing and co-creation of hetero-glossic perspectives during a time of disconnectivity; or they can be ostensibly convivial platforms 'used to disguise racism, sexism, and commercial or even exploitative relations'.

On a more structural level, translation can serve as a method for communication. Relevant here is the work of Guobin Yang (2020), who adopts a translation lens to rethink the assumptions in communication studies. Whereas prevailing views of communication place a premium on commonality and solidarity, translation foregrounds difference and negotiation, entailing 'an attitude of openness and re-ceptive[ness] to new experiences, new values, and new ways of doing things' (188). For Yang, the to-and-fro movement between self and other inherent in translation, manifested as 'a pedagogy of practice, revision, adjustment, and attunement' (187), makes it a valuable me-taphor for communication. This conception of translation as an open-ended site of engagement with alterity dovetails into the related ideas of linguistic hospitality (Ricoeur), dialogism (Bakhtin), translation-as-listening (Rabassa) and storytelling as an exchange of experiences (Benjamin). The notion of communication-as-translation thus reverses the unilateral disposition of communication, inflecting the latter with a dynamic based on 'difference, dialogue, receptivity, mutual change, and self-transformation':

> [A] view of communication as translation, as opposed to a view of communication as transmission, community, or ritual, is premised on the recognition of difference, dialogue, receptivity, mutual change, and self-transformation. This view of communication as translation has important ethical and practical implications for the practice of communication research, indeed, for any practices of knowledge production.
>
> (Yang 2020: 190)

Building on this, **José van Dijck** and **Donya Alinejad** use translation as a heuristic to theorize on two models of *knowledge translation*, using as their case study the Netherlands's public debate on COVID-19 measures during which health information is mediated among policy-makers, scientists, journalists and the non-expert public. The first is the institutional model, which 'assumes linear vectors "transmitting" information from experts to nonexperts'. This model postulates point-to-point trajectories of health-related knowledge from science professionals to policy-makers and from policy-makers to the public via legacy as well as social media. Its unidirectionality speaks to the prevailing paradigm of communication based on 'transmission, community, or ritual', which Yang (cited above) deems in need of revision. In contrast to this, and corresponding to the communication-as-translation paradigm, is what **van Dijck** and **Alinejad** term the networked model, one that 'incorporates social media as a centrifugal force, changing the dynamics of information exchange conceptually from "transmission" to "translation"'.

In the Netherlands, the institutional model was evident in the early 'crisis response' phase where the government managed the exigencies of the virus situation by channelling expert opinion to the public in a top-down fashion. This was complemented by the networked model, which entered the scene in the subsequent 'smart exit strategy' stage, where scientists and policy-makers adapted 'their strategies by *translating* information to various target groups and through different channels, allowing more types of arguments and rendering the debate between officials and citizens more dialogic' (emphasis added). This transition from the institutional to the networked model, premised on translation as a favourable metaphor for the negotiation of difference, can be mapped onto developments in translation studies itself. It is a commonplace that our understanding of translation has shifted from static, linguistics-based models that foreground the linearity of source-to-target relationships, to dynamic, communication-based models that privilege transformations over transference. **Van Dijck** and **Alinejad** exemplify this development in the domain of social media communication, bringing into relief the intralingual and interdiscursive rather than translingual dimension of translation, which mediates the flows of health information across diverse demographics in a nation.

Yet the 'translational' networked model, as empowered by social media, is not a panacea either. As **van Dijck** and **Alinejad** astutely observe, social media are inherently capricious platforms, 'two-sided swords of health communication'. While facilitating egalitarian flows of information, they are subject to market forces and vulnerable to being weaponized by internet celebrities in subverting authentic knowledge regimes and jeopardizing public trust in legacy media. In the final analysis, the networked model transforms, but does not displace, the institutional model. As the pandemic continues to unravel, both models have a distinct role to play at different stages in the management of health communications, demanding that policy-makers and professional communicators modulate flexibly between transmission and translation.

(A)symmetries and (dis)trust: Translation as communication

From communication-as-translation, we now turn to translation-as-communication in which translation takes on a more substantive sense. In the crisis context of COVID-19, effective translation is an integrated solution for communicating public health exigencies among different languages connecting various parties, including members of affected communities, responders and crisis managers on site, media personnel and policy-makers. Yet due to the unequal distribution of linguistic capital across urban demographics, translation is often asymmetrical, or even altogether absent. Observing the semiotic landscape in London of early 2020, Zhu (2021: 48) notes the relative paucity of multilingualism in shop signage providing information on exigent measures:

> The lack of public information in other languages is a particular concern when so much depends on the public understanding and complying with the rules and the regulations. What does the new vocabulary, with words such as 'lockdown', 'social distancing', 'self-isolation' and 'face covering' (which is not equivalent to 'face mask')—terms that were not part of our daily conversation before the pandemic but which now we can now say in one breath—mean in other cultures and other languages? And how do the people who speak other languages figure out the degree of obligation in the government's key messages and directives?

This non-availability of public information or critical terminology in languages other than English highlighted above is an issue of translation. It points to asymmetries in health communications that may have dire consequences for users of minority languages. This theme is taken up by **Renée Desjardins** in her case study of the Manitoban government's use of social media as part of its pandemic management.

What **Desjardins** finds in Manitoba is perhaps a classic problem with top-down communication in culturally and linguistically diverse (CALD) peoples, namely the privileging of official languages—French and English in this case—in the dissemination of COVID-related information; and, as a corollary, the lack of interest, let alone concerted effort, in translating said information into languages that fall outside the official matrix, as in Canada's Aboriginal and immigrant languages. At stake here is the tension between the 'logic of official languages' and *translational justice* in the time of crisis. Translational injustice occurs when critical information on government social media platforms is provided only in the official languages, thus implicitly discriminating against segments of the population who use only or predominantly the community languages. This has serious implications for equitable accessibility to public health resources that is so crucial during COVID-19, essentially creating 'an asymmetry in actionable knowledge' around disparities in linguistic capital. Nontranslation can therefore exacerbate existing social and economic inequities developed along the faultlines of languages, such as Canada's 'bilingual belt'.

The inadequacies of official translation strategies in respect of pandemic communications raise the question of trust, an especially sensitive issue in times of crisis, particularly in superdiverse settings. For users of community languages, social media serve as the go-to source of updated information in their mother tongues. This could be because, as related in **Desjardins**'s Manitoba case, translation into community languages is altogether lacking. Or, as **Sharon O'Brien**, **Patrick Cadwell** and **Tetyana Lokot** find from, inter alia, their interviews of Brazilian migrant workers in Ireland, among others, social media constitute a 'parallel online space' in which these foreign residents seek not just information but also emotional refuge. Where information from state sources is needed, these workers may seek recourse to Google Translate to help them understand the messages in their home languages, even if there is a degree of mistrust in translation technology for this purpose.

Translated communication in social media therefore participates in a political economy of marginalization and resistance. It plays out 'the logic of "us", particularly within CALD communities, against "them" in power', which, as **Anthony Pym** and **Bei Hu** tell us, pivots these communities from trusting science and official media to trusting community agents and social media. In this regard, it is found that professional translation, for instance as commissioned by the state, does not always have a major role to play in the context of COVID communications, reversing the conventional wisdom that nonprofessional translators are generally less trustable in crisis settings (**O'Brien**, **Cadwell** and **Lokot**). Indeed, the ethical codes binding professional translators may conflict with what is required of them during the exigencies of a health crisis. For example, the AUSIT Code of Ethics and Code of Conduct[3] governing translators in Australia stipulates the principle of professional detachment and impartiality, requiring that translators refrain from roles 'offering advocacy, guidance, or advice'.[4] Pym (2020) remarks that such a principle does not fit well in a pandemic context, where 'building trust is vital if the aim is to achieve understanding and cooperation', thus demanding a more diffusive kind of translation that blurs into such services as advocacy, guidance or advice. Accuracy, the key criterion for professional translation, no longer suffices on its own in COVID settings. Of equal—dare we say greater—importance is the degree to which the source (as opposed to the content) of information is trusted by intended users (**O'Brien, Cadwell** and **Lokot**).

Thus, to ease a populace into the new normal, entailing collective changes in proxemics (social distancing), health-related apparel (face masks) and hygiene rituals (hand sanitizing), the community at large would need to trust the source of information in the first place. In this connection, effective communication, measurable by the degree to which it induces desirable changes in collective behaviour, is no longer pre-mised on the representation of truth or reality. It becomes a type of performative simulacra, à la Baudrillard, whereby the discursive per-formance of a represented entity or event ensues in action. In the case of translated communication, then, we have *translational simulacra* based on multiple retellings in different languages, which further complicates the issue of trust with risk. Choosing a course of action on the basis of information translated from an unfamiliar language and a culture always involves 'risk-based trust', as **Pym** and **Hu** remind us, because of the 'fewer shared referents' across the linguistic threshold, leading to 'greater risks of disbelief, denial, and dissent'. And what happens if trust falters? Because distrust of translation 'is a particularly corrosive solvent' of translational simulacra, a breakdown of trust in translated commu-nications would likely frustrate systemic efforts in promoting collective behavioural change in CALD communities.

Amid this subtle shift in trust dynamics, social media have engendered a decentring and de-professionalization of translation, a development that did not begin with the pandemic for sure, but is nonetheless ac-centuated by it. In social media, trust is turned on its head, as Botsman (2017: 8) would have it, enabling certain nonexpert voices to attract symbolic authority through multimodal postings, as well as the 'friends', followings, likes, shares, retweets and recommendations attracted by these postings (**van Dijck** and **Alinejad**). For example, in circumstances where official health communication is not readily accessible by users of minority languages due to non-translation, micro-influencers enter to bridge the information gap via social media (**O'Brien, Cadwell** and **Lokot**). These micro-influencers typically share identity resources with targeted audiences in the community, affording them a credibility capital to serve as quasi-translators or citizen journalists on popular platforms such as YouTube, WhatsApp and WeChat. These platforms not only provide translations of authorized information from institutional sources; they are also sites of cultural belonging within CALD and diasporic communities. By opening up a 'third cultural space' for participants to express their views during difficult times, and at times inflecting translated journalistic information with language-specific memes, these popular sites contribute to 'shap[ing] the formation of a hybridized cultural identity and prompt[ing] active communication' (**Pym** and **Hu**).

Yet there is a dark side to these non-institutionalized, trust-based channels of translation. For one thing, micro-influencers operating on a mercenary basis can switch their loyalties between government and anti-government sources depending on who is sponsoring their channel, thus potentially exposing the public to conflicting information (**van Dijck** and **Alinejad**). The circumvention of professional translation also creates the risk of mistranslation and misinformation. Given these issues, the best way forward is for authorities to synergize top-down and bottom-up communication efforts by co-opting trust-based translation, such that trust-building is executed 'as a form of preparedness' (**O'Brien**, **Cadwell** and **Lokot**). This may take the form of policy changes, such as allocating funding to community bodies with access to popular platforms, as a way to boost their resources for translation (**Pym** and **Hu**). It can also involve identifying 'trusted voices as micro-influencers within communities' (**O'Brien**, **Cadwell** and **Lokot**) and preparing them to translate official health information competently and responsibly to these communities. Translation, in other words, cannot be an afterthought in pandemic management (**Desjardins**).

After #COVID-19

Together the authors mentioned above have shown how information is negotiated, translated and distorted across different social groups and media platforms. Social media provide essential forums for such participation (or transgression) based on the fluid relations among producers, translators and users of online information. Rather than generating clusters of transient, one-way communications, these platforms create information networks in response to the habits and preferences of the specified users, although apparently egalitarian, rhizomatic social media platforms can turn out to be non-neutral sites of ideological contestation. Meanwhile, the exploitation of social media potentialities for communication has an unprecedented impact on media ecology and the human world at large.

Moving forward, translation theory and praxis will continue to explore the new media literacies and social media technologies that translators and interpreters can integrate into multilingual contexts of crisis management. What comes to the fore is the relation between translation and technology against the backdrop of a perpetual health crisis and, more broadly, in the age of the Anthropocene. Translation motivates a spirit of collaboration between the platformization of Internet media (van Dijck et al. 2018) and the creative power of human-based communications. As Michael Cronin (2017: 102) observes, '[a] political ecology of translation technology must critically evaluate the resource implications of current uses of technology and advance alternative scenarios for the development of the translation cyborg in the age of the Anthropocene'. This is accentuated in a pandemic context, which urges us to respond to the pressing need for translators who can bridge gaps between languages and cultures by working with rather than against new technologies in search for opportunities to communicate their implications to the people whose surrounding realities, choices and lives are increasingly conditioned by their daily experiences on digital platforms.

In her ruminative piece, **Susan Bassnett** rides on Cronin's thinking on eco-translation to provoke that we are compelled to rely more on digital technology to sustain connection and sociability in a world stranded in the 'in-between state of consciousness'. As the coronavirus is transforming from the ground up the natural and artificial ecosystems on earth, the anthropocentric ecology has been so radically translated by the microbe that we can no longer carry on with everyday life as usual in this time of epochal change. Millions around the globe are 'still connected to the way in which they lived in pre-pandemic periods and yet negotiating how to move forward and "translate" themselves in a post-pandemic world'. The use of social media enhances COVID-safe communication but simultaneously threatens the prospect of an eco-friendly information society. **Bassnett** asks 'what might be the potential role of translators in the new world order to help rebuild confidence in human relationships, especially since the months of the pandemic have seen much greater prominence given to machine translation?' On this question she seems to lean towards a pessimistic stance.

We share **Bassnett**'s concerns that the post-COVID world may become one characterized by increased human-machine rather than human-human contact, including via translation. Taking cue from

Cronin (2013), however, we are also inclined to believe in the possibility of avoiding 'the dual dangers of terminal pessimism and besotted optimism by examining closely what is happening in today's translation world' (3). Translation can be 'a strategy of survival' through which we become different persons in times of crisis (**Vidal** and **Stavans**). It is also an essential anchor of plurality where diverse voices coming from different epistemological standpoints crisscross each other to enrich the fabric of our cultural and technological selves. As an 'ever-changing, self-renewing figure', translation points to 'the progenerative potential of the global, digital community to allow for the emergence of new forms of expression and engagement' (Cronin 2013:141). In facilitating the circulation of information, it aligns with 'the circulatory possibilities of the internet' and partakes of 'a programme of cultivation and understanding of the multiple perspectives of others' (Cronin 2017: 95). As **Bassnett** indicates, translation studies will continue to fulfil the mission of breaking down divisions and restoring culture after COVID.

In the post-pandemic milieu, translation studies will need to reorient itself in relation to emerging borders of all kinds—between geographical regions, states, nationalities, races, genders, ages and classes (**Bassnett**)—and continue to explore new, uncharted frontiers opened up by the pandemic in our information society. More broadly speaking, the humanities will have much to learn and more to teach about the culture of connectivity that involves 'the social, cultural, political and economic factors affecting the interaction of humans with other humans, other organisms and the physical environment' (Cronin 2017: 2). And it is in this context that the present volume endeavours to serve as a timely intervention in making preliminary observations, throwing up pertinent questions, and probing the way forward—even if we can never be translated back to the pre-COVID world again.

Notes

1 https://www.un.org/en/un-coronavirus-communications-team/un-tackling-%E2%80%98infodemic%E2%80%99-misinformation-and-cybercrime-covid-19
2 To avoid repetition of the phrase 'in this volume', hereafter the names of authors featured in this collection are bolded; quotations without page numbers are extracted from the chapters contained in this book, as indicated by author names.
3 https://www.2m.com.au/wp-content/uploads/2017/03/Code_Of_Ethics_Full.pdf
4 See Principle 6.1 under 'Obligation towards recipients of services', AUSIT Code of Ethics and Code of Conduct (ibid.).

References

Agamben, G. (2020). 'L'invenzione di un'epidemia', *Quodlibet*, February 26.
https://www.quodlibet.it/giorgio-agamben-l-invenzione-di-un-epidemia

Botsman, R. (2017). *Who Can You Trust? How Technology Brought Us Together and Why It Could Drive Us Apart*, New York: Penguin.

Cronin, M. (2013). *Translation in the Digital Age*, Abingdon: Routledge.

Cronin, M. (2017). *Eco-Translation: Translation and Ecology in the Age of the Anthropocene*, Abingdon: Routledge.

Pym, A. (2020). 'When trust matters more than translation', *Pursuit* (29 July),
https://pursuit.unimelb.edu.au/articles/when-trust-matters-more-than-translation

Van Dijck, J., Poell, T., and de Waal, M. (2018). *The Platform Society: Public Values in a Connective World*, New York: Oxford University Press.

Yang, G. (2020). 'Communication as translation: Notes toward a new conceptualization of communication', in M. Powers and A. Russell (Eds.), *Rethinking Media Research for Changing Societies*, Cambridge: Cambridge University Press, 184–194.

Zhu, H. (2021). 'Sense and sensibility: Urban public signs during a pandemic', in R. Jones (Ed.), *Viral Discourse*, Cambridge: Cambridge University Press, 37–48.

1 Cabin'd, Cribbed, Confin'd

How the COVID-19 pandemic is changing our world

Susan Bassnett

> *I had else been perfect,*
> *Whole as the marble, founded as the rock,*
> *As broad and general as the casing air;*
> *But now I am cabin'd, cribbed, confin'd, bound in*
> *To saucy doubts and fears.*
>
> (*Macbeth*, Act III, Scene IV)

Restricted mobility in times of the COVID-19 pandemic

In his book *Eco-Translation*, Michael Cronin makes a strong case for the global significance of a notion of translation that takes into account 'the social, cultural, political and economic factors affecting the interaction of humans with other humans, other organisms and the physical environment' (Cronin 2017: 2). He argues that we have been living in a time when ends have predominated over means, and suggests that the key issues for the twenty-first century which need to be addressed by everyone regardless of their subject affiliation include '[f]ood security, climate justice, biodiversity loss, water depletion, energy security, linguicide [the elimination of smaller languages by the more powerful ones], eco-migration, resource conflicts, [and] global monocultures' (3). Translation studies, a field that looks at how languages move around the world, cannot but engage with what he argues is a shift taking place across the sciences, social sciences and humanities. In the chapter entitled 'The Great Transition', Cronin looks at some of the vast planetary changes in communication of the last few years and comments pointedly that although the digital may deliver information across the planet in seconds, if the language is different, then there can be no valid communication. In a multilingual world, translation is the essential and vital companion of global outreach.

DOI: 10.4324/9781003183907-2

Since *Eco-Translation* came out in 2017, we have all witnessed unprecedented changes in our lives. Early in 2020 the pandemic caused by the coronavirus began to spread across the world. Since then, millions have found themselves confined in their own homes, some unable to go outside for weeks, some under curfew, and many forbidden to meet members of their own family for months on end. This mass global confinement of people across the world which has continued into 2021 came about through circumstances completely beyond anyone's control. Suddenly unable to move freely in a world where international mobility is highly prized and forced into confinement without prior warning, millions of people have had to adjust to an immense and disturbing change of circumstances. Trying to think in translational terms, it would appear that millions of people now find themselves in an in-between state of consciousness, still connected to the way in which they lived in pre-pandemic periods and yet negotiating how to move forward and 'translate' themselves in a post-pandemic world.

As I write, we still have no clear indication of how long this pandemic will last. Different parts of the world have been affected differently, so the figures of those who have contracted the disease and the numbers of deaths are wildly divergent. Some states like New Zealand, Australia, Vietnam and Taiwan moved quickly to close their borders, and so managed to keep the number of cases down, which was impossible in areas such as Europe where the borders are porous, or in those parts of the world where millions live in extreme poverty. Moreover, the medical crisis swiftly became politicized. Some heads of state initially underestimated the severity of the pandemic and made dismissive public statements. In some countries the provision of protective clothing for medical staff, hospital availability and the provision of vaccines proved inadequate, while in others there continues to be strong resistance to any vaccination programme. Conspiracy theories abound on the internet, and since the first outbreak appears to have been in Wuhan in China, one such theory claims that the spread of the disease was a deliberate act on the part of the Chinese government. In Europe, the animosity caused by the United Kingdom leaving the European Union has continued through arguments about the availability of vaccines and the very different speed at which different countries embarked on vaccination programmes.

There have been other pandemics, of course, but the global scale of this one makes it different from previous times. At the end of the First World War there were some 500 million people affected by the Spanish flu. Deaths were estimated at well over 50 million and the disease adversely attacked the young, with the majority of fatalities aged between 20 and 40. Other pandemics, though severe, affected particular parts of the world only. The SARS epidemic of 2003 was experienced mainly in Asia, while the Ebola epidemic of 2014–16 affected tens of thousands of people in Africa. What makes the COVID-19 case different is that the disease has spread so rapidly across the world, facilitated by what to date has been seen as a sign of twenty-first century progress—the ease of international mobility. COVID-19 is also a disease that appears to affect the older population more seriously, and given that another sign of progress in the developed world is the extension of life span, this means that a high number of fatalities are in the older age bracket.

After the end of the Cold War, the abolition of apartheid and China's opening up to the rest of the world, all of which happened in the early 1990s, millions of people who had previously been unable to travel acquired passports. This fact, combined with their changing economic circumstances, such as the emergence of a middle class in China and former Soviet-controlled countries, meant that international travel became the new reality for many. A mass global tourism boom started, and international travel, once the privilege of the wealthy few, became an everyday expectation. Business travel became the norm for hundreds of thousands of office workers whose parents had merely commuted into cities closer to home. Cruise ships—vast floating skyscraper palaces—along with budget airlines offered the promise of visits to exotic places to people who had previously only dreamed of such adventures, often older and more prosperous members of society. The abrupt end in 2020 to the kind of international travel to which millions in the developed world had become accustomed came as a shock, underlining perceptions of the severity of the pandemic and heightening anxiety for the future.

The cessation of most international travel in 2020 was inevitably combined with many countries closing their borders. Yet, open borders with freedom of movement across national frontiers had been seen as another sign of twenty-first century progress, but the pandemic changed all that. In Europe, the Schengen agreement implemented in 1995 had guaranteed passport-free travel between those states which agreed to sign up to it, though Britain and Ireland were not Schengen signatories. The response of many of the Schengen countries, however, was to close borders and restrict travel in an attempt to control the spread of the virus. Moreover, despite the hopes of the European Union to establish a Europe-wide vaccination strategy, the acquisition of vaccines was problematic and led to individual nation states establishing their own systems, using different vaccines and targeting different members of the population. Early in 2021 Hungary became the first European nation to approve both the Russian and Chinese vaccines, an action that showed a widening gap in national policies within the European Union.

With borders closed, international travel banned and movement within countries severely restricted, the only solution available became electronic forms of communication. New systems proliferated for use in private, business and educational environments, the latter one was especially important as in many countries schools were closed for months and universities across the world ceased operating normally from the onset of the pandemic early in 2020. One of the most widely used systems is Zoom, developed by Zoom Video Communications founded in 2011 by a former employee of Cisco Webex, Eric Yuan. The company experienced a global boom as the pandemic took hold. So powerful is the use of Zoom that it has led to terminological changes with the invention of a transitive verb in English, 'to zoom'.

Technologies and changing communication systems

Yet communicating via Zoom raises some interesting questions that we will all need to think harder about as we move into a post-pandemic world. Although Zoom and other similar platforms make it possible for meetings to be held, for classes to be taught, and for conferences to take place with participants from many countries joining in, communicating electronically is not the same as communicating in the same physical environment. The information we have to date is anecdotal rather than scientifically demonstrable, but there is a generally held impression that working online via Zoom is exhausting. With systems like Zoom, there seems to be a degree of concentration that is more demanding than face-to-face encounters and in consequence behavioural patterns have altered. Online, normal patterns of conversation are not working in quite the same way as before. Turn-taking is different, for example. Either there are awkward silences at the start of a meeting when nobody is quite sure whether to speak, or people interrupt and talk over one another.

For teachers and academics, it is also much more difficult to gauge the impact of one's teaching on a virtual audience. In the classroom, one can sense shifts of energy, and during a lecture, for example, a teacher can tell if he or she has lost the attention of an audience when they start to cough, shuffle in their seats, or consult their mobile phones. In a meeting where the audience may be invisible there can be no sense of the impact one is making on an audience. Delia Chiaro, world expert on the problems of translating humour, told me personally that she had observed how Zoom killed the spontaneity of humour, an opinion corroborated by several other colleagues.

There is also an impression of heightened anxiety around Zoom meetings. This may be in part due to the unreliability of technology, particularly if the event involves a lot of people logging in from different places. But apart from that, the format itself seems to generate greater uneasiness. So we have the paradox that the very systems we are using in order to communicate electronically are heightening the anxiety caused by the spread of the pandemic. This is, of course, the antithesis of translation, where the aim is to make what is inaccessible or unclear in one context become available to a target audience in another.

In February 2021 the University of Glasgow conducted a survey among all university staff, sending out a series of questions relating to working from home and wellbeing. Other universities and places of work have conducted similar surveys in an endeavour not only to learn about the immediate effects of working from home, but also to see if there might be hints for the future. Over 2,000 people responded to the Glasgow survey, the majority of whom were working from home and overall, there was a high degree of satisfaction with the general level of communication and resources available provided by the university. However, although the response to the question about the effectiveness of working from home was positive for the most part, responses to other questions were very different. In response to a question asking about the impact of working from home personally, the majority said they felt isolated from colleagues, that there had been a negative impact on their mental health, that they found it difficult to step away from work at the end of the working day and that they would welcome a return to old working patterns. When the respondents were asked to list the main challenges of working from home, the issues highlighted in order of priority were difficulty in setting and maintaining boundaries; lack of communication with colleagues; increased workload; lack of appropriate working environment; lack of appropriate equipment; balancing work and caring responsibilities and difficulties of focus and motivation. Two-thirds of the respondents listed these as their principal concerns, with well over 75% indicating that they had difficulty setting and maintaining boundaries. Further down the list of their priorities, a third of respondents stated that adapting to the use of new IT skills was a problem, while poor quality of internet and telephone connections was listed by slightly more people. In response to the question about whether people might wish to work from home after lockdown regulations are lifted, the majority said they would settle for staying at home just two or three days a week, with 30% advocating a return to the workplace full time. There was clearly a desire for changes to working practice that might involve a combination of working from home and working *in situ*, though obviously those people whose research is laboratory-based constitute the majority of the percentage surveyed who found home working less than ideal.

Of course there are bound to be behavioural and linguistic changes that accompany technological developments as cultures adjust to new circumstances. In German, for example, the standard farewell greeting, *Auf wiedersehen* (Until we see each other again) became *Auf wiederhoeren* (Until we hear one another again) with the advent of the telephone. The arrival of email altered the traditional English forms of letter writing, so that instead of beginning a message with 'Dear x', some senders use an oral form of greeting such as 'Hello' or 'Hi' which suggests that the status of an email is not quite the same as that of a letter. An email may function in the same way as a letter in that it conveys information, but there is an impression that as a mode of communication it is less formal, closer to the spoken rather than to the written. This is reinforced by a shift in expectations: emails demand a faster response from the receiver. Failure to respond promptly to an email will often elicit a follow-up, putting pressure on the receiver to reply at once. This subtly alters the relationship between sender and receiver, creating an impression of inequality between the pursuer and the pursued which heightens stress levels for both parties.

Marshall McLuhan, the Canadian philosopher and communication theorist who died in 1980, argued that human beings are shaped by the technologies they invent. A new medium, he suggested, can reshape our lives, so that just as the advent of printing altered consciousness in the Western world, electronic media would bring about the advent of what he termed 'the global village' (McLuhan 1962). It may well be that as the world turns increasingly to electronic communication systems as a result of the pandemic, we are all somehow involved in another not yet fully understood process of reshaping consciousness.

Marshall McLuhan also advised that with technological changes that appear to enhance our living conditions comes obsolescence. His concern here was with the speed of change and the impact that change has on established systems and assumptions:

> Any new technique or idea or tool, while enabling a new range of activities by the user, pushes aside the older ways of doing things.

Money speeds transactions and gives rise to uniform pricing systems, obsolescing haggle and barter and much of the human relation to commodities. The motor car enhances private mobility, and pushes aside the old organization of the city in favour of the suburb.

(McLuhan and Zingrone 1997: 372)

Marshall McLuhan had died before the age of the internet began to develop globally, but his insistence on the fact that technologies reshape the world was ahead of his time. Reading his work today we can see the importance he attached to temporal changes—the accelerated speed of contemporary life, and the rapidly shifting cycles of obsolescence and retrieval. In the 'Introduction' of a posthumous collection of McLuhan's writings, the editors emphasize another aspect of his work, which they term the 'retribalization' of the structures of psychic and social awareness. What they mean by this term is that new communication technologies can easily become systems of control, and we can see this happening if we pause to think of the power wielded today by systems such as Facebook, Google, Twitter, etc. Mass censorship is a reality which we all experience, whether imposed by governments or by social media, and the fear generated by the pandemic serves to heighten this situation. Explaining Marshall McLuhan's concerns about societies becoming more divisive, Eric McLuhan and Frank Zingrone present a vision of the world that many of us today will recognize:

The Global Village of corporate consumer values stimulates local peoples to retrieve who they used to be as a protection for their fading identities, for electric process makes us all nobodies desperate for identity. The quest for identity, he warned, always produces violence. The old sensibility, old values, old enmities prevail over larger-scale democratic awareness and commitment.

(McLuhan and Zingrone 1997: 4)

This might seem to be an apocalyptic vision of a world changing with the increase of technological innovation, but what has become apparent is an increase of violence online. Old enmities are resurfacing, political and religious extremism is on the rise again, and social media is awash not only with conspiracy theories but with violent, aggressive attacks on individuals and groups. Cloaked by anonymity, anyone can launch an attack without fear of repercussion. In *13 Perspectives on the Pandemic: Thinking in a State of Exception*, a pamphlet published by De Gruyter in 2020, the German political scientist Marc Grimm discusses the rise of antisemitism during the pandemic. He notes the dissemination of conspiracy thinking generally, and then makes a direct connection with antisemitism:

> Everywhere we find this kind of 'alternative knowledge', with antisemitism just a small number of clicks away. The number of people who (sometimes unwillingly) fabricate their own partisan information through social media is growing. Those people are now starting to follow prominent conspiracy theorists on social media, and will continue to get their information through these channels in post-coronavirus times. And as the channels grow the algorithms of social media providers will suggest them to a wider audience.
>
> (Grimm 2020: 33)

Grimm has touched on something intangible yet enormously important here. If people are unable to engage in everyday conversational exchanges with others during periods of lockdown, isolation can lead to disproportionate fears that may be quickly translated into aggression and feelings of paranoia. The heightened emotive language online and in the media more generally reinforces this situation. Distinct tribes characterized by that heightened language and by expressions of greater aggression are indeed emerging. Every day, casual contact in the streets, workplaces, schools and universities is an essential and integral part of learning: people at work can share complaints, ideas and hypotheses over a cup of coffee or in a corridor; trainees can learn by watching how more expert colleagues behave and interact; employees can meet after work in informal environments to share thoughts about what has gone on during the day; and parents waiting at the school gate can exchange advice about their children and compare notes. Lockdowns have removed such casual contacts, increasing the sense of isolation in an individual and heightening doubts and anxieties. Even as the familiar structures of everyday life start to return, the experience that people have lived through means that they will see the world through different eyes, and one wonders how easily such life-enhancing casual contacts will return, given the undercurrents of violence and division that have been flowing through societies during the pandemic. A question to be asked is what might be the potential role of translators in the new world order to help rebuild confidence in human relationships, especially since the months of the pandemic have seen much greater prominence given to machine translation. Given that machine translation practice is much cheaper, we might consider whether this tendency is likely to continue into the future. Before the pandemic struck, back in 2019 the US economist Richard Baldwins published *The Globotics Upheaval*, a book which offered a dystopian vision of a future where face-to-face contact was radically diminished. Might the increased use of machine translation become a further step along that pathway?

Repercussions of the pandemic

Translation studies has been a field that has sought to break down divisions, cross over between languages and cultures, and highlight the importance of borderlessness. Now translation studies will need to position itself in a post-pandemic world where borders of all kinds are being constructed—between geographical regions, states, nationalities, races, genders, ages and classes. In *Eco-Translation* Cronin acknowledges the problem of what he calls the 'ontological fixation' which sees language practice as being about one language or another. 'A political ecology of translation', he states, 'views languages in their connectedness not in their isolation' (Cronin 2017: 152). And supporting what he terms 'an ecological championing of language diversity' that eschews binary oppositions, he goes on to say that:

> Notions of translanguaging or metrolingualism are in a sense an attempt to capture that transitional nature of the *inter*, of the silent transformation which characterises translation in the movement between and through language and context.
>
> (Cronin 2017: 152 original emphasis)

With the emergence of new physical and psychological borders that reinforce the pre-existing borders of the pre-pandemic world, to what extent the progress made towards greater connectedness will be set back now is a question that we need to ask. For those of us hoping to resume our lives of teaching and research, the sense of doubt and ambiguity is all too evident. Libraries have been closed and classrooms have remained empty, but humanities researchers have managed to cope with this, since unlike those colleagues who need laboratories for the advancement of their research, they are able to work from their own homes. Already, though, concerns are starting to be expressed about the future of research culture in the humanities. Doris Bachmann-Medick sees the pandemic as having not only narrowed the range of topics featuring in public discourse but also reduced the complexity of discussions. She is fearful as to whether this narrowing will further reduce funding opportunities in the humanities as attention shifts to highlighting the importance of research in virology, medicine, epidemiology and biotechnology. The global research environment has contracted during the pandemic, and Bachmann-Medick worries that humanities disciplines, which question and challenge received wisdom, will be the biggest losers. But she makes a strong case for the importance of the humanities and of cultural studies in particular in the new, post-pandemic world precisely because it is here that questions can be asked about shifts in power relations that have been taking place during the pandemic, about changes to the regulation of public and private spaces and about the ways in which different cultures have perceived and dealt with the crisis.

Bachmann-Medick insists on the need for the humanities to hold onto their critical perspective, even if research funding is reduced in a post-pandemic world. The virus has brought about great changes that we are just beginning to see, but she proposes that we all need to be open to the challenges that such changes will bring:

> The corona crisis has certainly brought about such a metamorphosis of the world. But it's a metamorphosis that isn't only disruptive: it is also a constructive challenge to overcome received ideas and supplant them with new ones. The humanities, with their emphasis on critically interrogating historical and social circumstances, can not only provide new ways of thinking in the post-corona era, but also point us towards new ways of acting. One thing is for sure: the corona crisis will usher research in the humanities into new, uncharted territory.
>
> (Bachmann-Medick 2020: 82–83)

Coping with isolation: An eighteenth-century example

However, coping with isolation is not just a twenty-first century problem. There is a long tradition of prison literature by people shut off from the world and trying to explain their thought processes during confinement. One notable example is the short work by the French aristocrat Xavier de Maistre published in 1794, entitled *Voyage autour de ma chambre*, translated into English by Henry Atwell in 1871 and more recently by Andrew Brown in 2004 as *A Journey around my Room*. In this work, de Maistre gives a parodic account of his 'journey' around a room in his house after being sentenced to 42 days of house arrest following a duelling incident. He sets out to systematically 'explore' his room, ironically recommending room travel to others as a cheap, uncomplicated way of discovering new territory, though of course that new territory is within himself. As he studies the contents of his room, his memory and imagination take him out into the world beyond physical confines, back in time through sequences of memories, interrupted only on such occasions as when he burns his hand while making toast. What de Maistre does is to show how, despite his confinement, the world is still accessible to him, albeit not in its physical reality. But towards the end of his journeying, when he learns that he is to be released, a sense of ambiguity creeps into his narrative. Protesting at the idea that freedom will be restored to him, he declares indignantly that nobody has the power to take his freedom away and 'to prevent me from exploring at will the vast space that always lies open before me!' (De Maistre 2013: 70). The life of the mind remains unchanged, and he asserts his right to inner freedom regardless of circumstances. But then, in his final paragraph he confesses to feeling 'double', which he explains as follows: 'a secret power draws me on; it tells me that I need the heaven's air, and that solitude resembles death' (71). He puts on his outdoor clothes, his door opens and he steps outside, but adds: 'I am filled with a premonitory shudder'. In his penultimate sentence he compares the ambiguity of his feelings to cutting into a lemon and feeling its acid taste already in his mouth. His final sentence is a warning—'Oh my beast, my poor beast, beware!' (71).

De Maistre recognizes that isolation from the world is double-edged. True, he has been able to amuse himself by virtual travel, by his memories and fantasies but he also recognizes that solitude resembles a kind of death. Going out and back into the world is not straightforward, as his experience of solitary confinement has changed him. He is more tentative, more anxious, even as he enjoys the fresh air and the agreeable phantoms that flutter before his eyes when he walks the streets and returns to human society. He is, as he states, 'double' and that sense of doubleness is a phenomenon being recorded anecdotally today, as people start to emerge from the months of lockdown imposed during the pandemic. Older people in particular, some of whom have been shut off in care homes or isolating at home, may never be sufficiently confident to re-engage with the world in the way they did before. One of the aftereffects of the pandemic could be greater divide between generations, with an older population more fearful and a younger generation, deprived of their education for so long, demonstrably angrier and more resentful with policy-makers.

Post-pandemic prospects

In 2020 the British Comparative Literature Association opened a forum on its website inviting contributions in response to the question as to whether culture might help people to cope with the unprecedented situation. In my contribution to the discussion, I pointed out that the aftermath of any catastrophe, whether war, revolution, natural disaster or plague, is never easily or quickly resolved. It takes time for radical changes to circumstances to be absorbed socially and for people to adjust to those changes (Bassnett 2021). As we come out of the pandemic, we will also need to turn our attention back to another global crisis, which has tended to be neglected through the COVID crisis: the question of climate change and the environment. Early in 2020 I started to notice changes in the atmosphere caused by a decline of polluting vehicles on land and in the air: visibility was enhanced, the stars at night shone more brightly, and sound seemed to carry further across the valleys. Studies suggest that the reduction of global and economic transport activity is leading to a reduction in air pollution (Venter et al. 2020). The authors of an article published in 2020 in *Proceedings of the National Academia of Sciences of the United States of America* came to this conclusion after studying air pollution in several countries as the lockdowns spread. What remains to be seen is whether this improvement will be temporary and disappear once international travel starts to increase again. Moreover, these more positive findings will have to be offset against the billions of masks, PPE, syringes and flow test kits, all of which put quantities of plastic back into the ecosystem and much of it is not recyclable.

De Maistre, imprisoned within the four walls of his own room, coped with his situation by allowing his imagination to travel out beyond those physical limitations. The present pandemic has led to another kind of confinement, as people across the world, innocent of any crime, find themselves unable to move about freely and, when they are once again allowed to move, will probably do so more hesitantly, with a previously unexperienced sense of anxiety. Moreover, the pandemic has raised important questions that remain to be answered: whether the scale of global travel will ever return to pre-pandemic levels, whether the current rise in the use of machine translation will affect those who earn a living as translators and interpreters, whether the extent to which we have deployed electronic communication systems will change how we communicate with one another, and how we teach and what kind of impact such changes may have on the learning process of future generations. Above all, in a world where old borders have been reimposed and new borders created, we need to ask whether we will see the reinforcement of borders become both a psychological and a physical reality, and if so, what the future for the millions of displaced people and migrants across the world might be.

At the start of this essay there is a quotation from Shakespeare's *Macbeth*, lines spoken when Macbeth realizes that he will be forever a prisoner of his own evil deeds. The three words, 'cabin'd, cribbed, confin'd' have come often into my mind since the spring of 2020 when the pandemic began to spread across the world. But unlike Macbeth who causes his predicament by his own wickedness, the confinement of people across the world in 2020 and 2021 has come about through circumstances beyond their individual control.

The global pandemic will have consequences for the future, quite apart from the damage it has inflicted on the physical and mental wellbeing of individuals, on world trade, on the economic health of nations, on up-and-coming generations whose education has been damaged and whose employment prospects have been blighted. It has called into question how we engage with the daily fabric of our society and is making us rethink how we communicate with one another. In the future, looking back, perhaps this fraught period may turn out to have been a profoundly significant year in the story of how human communication systems change and develop as circumstances force us to look differently at the world. Let us all hope that the changes will not be as dark as they appear right now.

References

Bachmann-Medick, D. (2020). 'The humanities—marginalized after corona?', in R. Rittgerodt (Ed.), *13 Perspectives on the Pandemic: Thinking in a State of Exception (A De Gruyter Humanities Pamphlet)*, Berlin: De Gruyter, 78–83.

Bassnett, S. (2021). The ploughshare and the needle: Reflections on culture in the age of confinement, *British Comparative Literature Association*, https://bcla.org/reflections/the-ploughshare-and-the-needle/

Cronin, M. (2017). *Eco-Translation: Translation and Ecology in the Age of the Anthropocene*, Abingdon and New York: Routledge.

De Maistre, X. (2013). *A Journey Around my Room*, trans. A. Brown, London: Alma Books.

Grimm, M. (2020). 'Antisemitism on social media in times of corona', in R. Rittgerodt (Ed.), *13 Perspectives on the Pandemic: Thinking in a State of Exception (A De Gruyter Humanities Pamphlet)*, Berlin: De Gruyter, 29–33.

McLuhan, E., and Zingrone, F. (Eds.). (1997). *Essential McLuhan*, London: Routledge.

McLuhan, M. (1962). *The Gutenberg Galaxy*, Toronto: University of Toronto Press.

Venter, Z. S., Aunan K., Chowdhury S., and Lelieveld, J. (2020). 'COVID-19 lockdowns cause global air pollution declines', *PNAS* 117(32): 18984–18990.

2 Translating Knowledge, Establishing Trust

The role of social media in communicating the COVID-19 pandemic in the Netherlands

José van Dijck and Donya Alinejad

Introduction

At a time of crisis, social media are a double-edged sword in health communication. They can be weaponized as conduits for misinformation and for undermining institutional and professional trust (Llewellyn 2020); at the same time, they can be utilized as valuable tools for public engagement and information distribution. Watching the corona pandemic unfold in 2020, we noticed how the epidemiology of the disease is intricately entwined with the epistemology of health communication and the practices of spreading reliable information (Bjørkdahl and Carlsen 2019). The higher stakes in this contested process prompt our two research questions central to this article: How are social media dynamics deployed to both undermine *and* enhance public trust in scientific expertise during a health crisis? And what does this mean for health communication as an intricate process of information exchange, public debate and knowledge translation?

To answer these questions, we first reflect in the second section on the notions of 'transmission' versus 'translation' in the process of health communication (Yang 2020). We will use these notions to discuss how, over the past few decades, science communication has shifted from an *institutional* model towards a *networked* model (Botsman 2017). Foregrounding the notion of communication as 'translation' we argue that in recent processes of health communication, social media have emerged as propellers of networked information flows rather than as instruments of top-down information transmission.

In the third and fourth sections, we use these two models of health communication to examine the role of social media in the public

DOI: 10.4324/9781003183907-3

debate involving scientists (experts), government (policy-makers), mass media (journalists) and citizens (non-experts) during the first four months after the COVID-19 outbreak in the Netherlands. Analysing this public exchange in two stages, we hypothesize that the networked model of science communication *transforms*, rather than replaces, the institutional model by adapting the logic and dynamics of social media to enhance institutional authority. We conclude by reflecting on what this transformation means for communication professionals trying to navigate between retaining institutional trust and adapting to divergent information flows in a volatile media landscape.

From an institutional to a networked model of health communication

For the past half century, science communication in Western-European societies has predominantly relied on a conventional model, characterized by linear flows of information between professional actors acting as gatekeeping forces. We trust science and scientists as institutions of knowledge-making; government and its (elected) officials as institutions of policy-making; and media and journalists as institutions of public sense-making. All three institutions are aimed at constructing common knowledge, common ground and common sense. The institutional model is grounded in shared assumptions on *whom* to trust, *what* to trust and *how* trust gets *built* (Oreskes 2019).

In theory, the institutional model of science communication assumes linear vectors 'transmitting' information from experts to non-experts: scientists provide governments with relevant information so they can make informed decisions, while policy-makers inform news media and the public about the rationale behind their decisions, fostering democratic, open debates (Figure 2.1). In practice, such a model has never manifested in its pure form; scientific knowledge-making and evidence-informed policy-making, rather than being linear transmissions of knowledge, have always been part of a dynamic process in which expert voices—framed by scientific, governmental and media institutions—get interwoven with non-expert voices in the struggle for public consent (Weingart and Joubert 2019; Schäfer 2016; Van Dijck 1995).

The institutional 'transmission' model has also prevailed in health communication, enhancing the ideal of institutional filters and gatekeepers as pillars of public trust. More recently, communication scholars have introduced the notion of 'translation' as a more relevant concept for public information exchange, emphasizing the need for

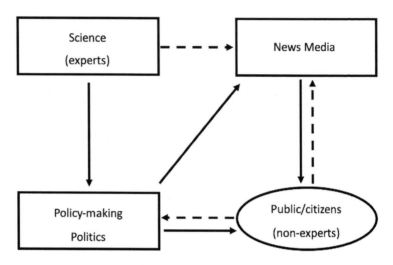

Figure 2.1 The institutional-transmission model of science communication.

new tropes in a rapidly changing media landscape. American media scholar Guobin Yang described the notion of translation as

> an ongoing conversation of learning, listening, and revision. It is dialogic and self-reflexive. Communicators often want to inform and enlighten others; translators must be prepared for self-enlightenment.
>
> (Yang 2020: 189)

The concept of translation regards communication no longer as a hierarchical and linear but as a dialogic and adaptive process. The concept of translation cannot be seen apart from the emergence of social media technologies gaining a central position in public communication in recent decades. According to Oxford economist Rachel Botsman, social media have allegedly 'turned trust on its head'; information that used to flow 'upwards to referees and regulators, to authorities and experts, to watchdogs and gatekeepers, is now flowing horizontally, in some instances to our fellow human beings and, in other cases, to programs and bots' (Botsman 2017: 8).

In contrast to the institutional-transmission model, we present the networked-translation model of health communication—a model that incorporates social media as a centrifugal force, changing the dynamics of information exchange conceptually from 'transmission' to 'translation'.

Experts and institutionally embedded health professionals no longer have a monopoly on informing politicians and mass media, as social media platforms afford every citizen and non-expert a communication channel. Non-expert voices gain clout through messages and videos they post, but also through the automated likes, shares, re-tweets and recommendations pushed by platforms; 'friends' and non-experts seem to be qualified to communicate information on par with institutions or experts. Slow-growing consensus based in fact-finding missions and processed through logical argument seems no longer the exclusive basis for 'evidence-informed' policy which in turn feeds mass media and the public debate. Rather, non-expert emotions, experience, sentiments, feelings and trends are distributed through social media and are processed algorithmically, affecting the information cycle in real time. The networked-translation model relies less on a one-to-many style of communication deploying text, context and logic to convince recipients, and more on a many-to-many style of communication that utilizes opinions, visuals, memes and short clips to mobilize crowds. As political economist William Davies (2018: 6) observes, 'information moves like a virus through a [social] network in far more erratic ways'. The circular vectors of information flows have been illustrated in Figure 2.2.

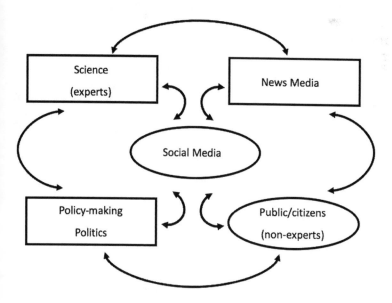

Figure 2.2 The networked-translation model of science communication.

This networked-translation model of science communication should be considered part of a wider transformation, where epistemic trust is at the heart of a socio-technical and a political power shift. In the twenty-first century, open democratic societies appear to be moving away from institutional-professional forms of trust towards networked-algorithmic forms of trust (Crawford 2019). The first is predicated on human-made rules of gate-keeping power governed by publicly accountable institutions and professionals, while the second one hinges on algorithmic filtering and is governed by proprietary business models, the dynamics of which are based on opaque rules (Van Dijck et al. 2018). And while the first model is informed mainly by concepts of top-down linear information transmission, the second one incorporates circular and dialogic communication modes. The convergence of these two models in a public debate prompts the question: How can social media be deployed to both undermine and enhance public trust in expertise during a health crisis?

A number of scholars have voiced their growing concerns about social media platforms undermining public trust, particularly with regards to the rise of disinformation and polarization. For instance, American communication theorist Zeynep Tufekçi (2019: n.p.) argues that 'the internet is increasingly a low-trust society—one where an assumption of pervasive fraud is simply built into the way many things function'. The shift away from the institutional model towards the networked model, according to Swedish media scholar Peter Dahlgren (2018), has led to a corrosion of trust that visibly affects *all* independent institutions entrusted with the anchoring of Western democratic values: science and health institutions, government agencies and news organizations. The question whether social media fuel institutional distrust or whether institutional distrust weaponizes social media has been at the core of scholars' concerns about fake news and disinformation years before the COVID-19 outbreak (Bradshaw and Howard 2018; Lazer et al. 2018; Benkler et al. 2018).

However, the idea of social media as agents of disinformation tends to obscure the underlying complexity involved in processes of knowledge-making, policy-making and sense-making. Particularly at the time of a health crisis, such as the COVID-19 pandemic, online platforms and social media can be regarded simultaneously as *levers of trust and distrust* in public debates. On the one hand, the proliferation of unfiltered voices through social media may cause a breakdown of trust in expert voices, officials and mainstream institutions, because 'the differentiation between individuals who are qualified to provide accurate information online and so-called armchair epidemiologists is increasingly difficult' (Limaye et al. 2020: E278). On the other hand, social media platforms give citizens a voice, providing a counterweight 'to the felt lack of fit between experience and what we are offered by the official organs, and a corollary lack of trust in them' (Crawford 2019: 92). Citizens and non-experts may rightly claim their place next to expert voices in the public debate, if only to promote the transparency and accountability of policy-making (Song and Lee 2015). Australian scholar Anthony Pym studied how social media helped facilitate communication between the state government, scientists and multilingual communities; he argues that understanding distrust among various cultural groups is essential if government officials want to finetune information about the COVID-19 measures for diverse recipients (Pym 2020).

Each of the two models represents a distinct perspective on how health information is communicated and each model follows a different pattern of distributing information (transmission versus translation). And yet, it would be misleading to argue that the two models are antithetical or mutually exclusive; it would also be a mistake to argue that the second model has replaced or is replacing the first, resulting in the deterioration of institutional trust per se. Instead, we hypothesize in this article that the two models operate concurrently and are mutually transforming one another. While social media platforms can be deployed to undermine public trust in institutions and expert knowledge, they are also used by authorities and communication experts to reach a widespread audience in order to retain trust. The concept of translation may help us understand how the latter can adjust their practices to do so.

Against the more general backdrop of this transforming media landscape, we now want to turn to a specific case of health communication by analysing the public debate that evolved in the Netherlands right after the COVID-19 outbreak, between 1 March and 30 June 2020.[1] We analysed this public debate in two phases. The first stage of this process, described in the following section, was characterized by the 'emergency response' to the hasty lockdown—a highly volatile period when controlling the health narrative was crucial (Weible 2020; Garrett 2020). While social media proliferated as conduits for misinformation and conspiracy theories about the virus, they also served as useful gateways to scientific information (Hagen et al. 2018). The second stage of the debate, analysed in the fourth section, shifted attention from the medical emergency response to the broader concern about a 'smart exit strategy' from the lockdown. Looking for new strategies, policy-makers started to engage with citizens and non-experts in the design of a post-corona society; by adapting net-working and crowdsourcing tactics, they strategically tried to retain institutional trust and legitimacy. Analysing this two-tiered debate, we try to show how social media dynamics are deployed in various ways to both undermine *and* enhance public trust in expertise during a health crisis.

The 'crisis response' stage

The government's decision to impose a lockdown on the country in response to the threat of an unknown virus, which had blown over from China and northern Italy before hitting the Netherlands in early March of 2020, was unprecedented. The first stage of this response was characterized by high volatility and uncertainty—a period when evidence-informed policy-making almost coincided with public sense-making, due to the intense time pressure under which these communication processes evolved. The most poignant concerns raised during this phase were: Is the government doing enough or overreacting? How were drastic measures communicated: were they 'transmitted' hierarchically to mass audiences or was health information gradually 'translated' to specific target groups and communities and adjusted accordingly?

When the first of the corona patients started to fill the hospital beds, the Prime Minister staged a press conference on 12 March that triggered intense reactions of anxiety and insecurity (Rijksoverheid.nl 2020). A sweeping package of containment measures was announced, including working from home for all non-essential professionals, no more crowd events and social distancing, but no complete enforced lockdown. Later that week, stricter measures were announced by ministers of health Bruno Bruins and Hugo de Jonge. On 15 March, Mark Rutte addressed the nation in a live speech—a first in history attracting 7 million viewers—in which he laid out three possible scenarios to fight the pandemic: (1) controlled spread, to avoid the overwhelming of the health system; (2) complete lockdown; and (3) uncontrolled spread. The government's choice for the first scenario, Rutte said, was based on scientific evidence informing this policy to reduce the number of deaths and minimize socio-economic impact while building up herd immunity: 'I don't expect people just trust their Prime Minister, but they have every reason to trust the experts'. In the days after the televised address, according to one poll, public trust in the government climbed to 73%, up from 45% (NPO1, 17 March, 2020).

At this first stage, the government highlighted rational explanation and reliance on trusted health experts—perfectly in line with the institutional model of health communication. News organizations (TV and print) followed suit by featuring mostly health specialists in their news reports on the measures. The debate about whether the government was overreacting or underestimating the pandemic happened mostly in the opinion sections of newspapers, talk shows and on social media platforms. Critical questions were raised concerning the effectiveness of herd immunity. Due to the international nature of the crisis and the global flows of online information, the difference between the Dutch response and measures taken by other governments sharply entered the debate, pressing policy-makers to clarify in the mainstream media and in Parliament that herd immunity was never meant to be a 'goal' in itself but a welcome 'side-effect' of the controlled spread policy. In both cases, policy adjustments were prompted by countervoices arguing that the government was not doing enough to stop the pandemic. At times of emergency management, policy-makers who are still used to one-directional dissemination of information were now exposed to 'vast amounts of information originating from the public' (Simon et al. 2015: 616), which they had to handle with care. Clearly, the government preferred 'imperfect policy-making' approved by public consent over 'perfect policy-making' causing public resistance and disapproval.

The emergency response also included strong initial warnings against untrustworthy information coming from unidentified sources, mostly through social media. Unsurprisingly, a barrage of misinformation and fake news had flooded individuals' Facebook news feeds, YouTube channels and Twitter feeds. The World Health Organization (WHO) quickly coined the term 'infodemic' to point at the 'overabundance of information—some accurate and some not—that makes it hard for people to find trustworthy sources and reliable guidance when they need it' (Wiederhold 2020: 1). False stories quickly went viral; for instance, advice falsely attributed to Stanford University stated that taking a few sips of warm water every 15 minutes was adequate prevention against infection. More dangerous were the numerous recommendations to drink pure alcohol, use a specific toothpaste, or drink bleach water. And downright rampant were the conspiracy theories that linked the spread of the coronavirus to the ultrafast wireless technology known as 5G. In less than two months, the Dutch police reported more than 25 incidents of vandalized telecom infrastructure, all connected to corona-related activists.

National and European governments quickly launched coordinated efforts to fight the infodemic (EU vs DiSiNFO 2020). Although social media platforms were not the exclusive distributors of misinformation—popular newspapers in the Netherlands also published sensational stories—the pressure to act responsibly as mediators of public information weighed heavily on their shoulders. After years of disputing social media platforms' inability to algorithmically filter out fake news and misinformation, on 17 March, a collaboration among the most popular social media platforms (Facebook, Instagram, Twitter, YouTube, Reddit and LinkedIn) announced global measures to curb the threat (NU.nl, 17 March, 2020). First, Facebook and YouTube started to collaborate with the WHO, the Rijksinstituut voor Volksgezondheid en Milieu (RIVM, the Dutch Institute for Public Health) and the Dutch government by linking users to official information as well as to specially produced video clips. Second, Facebook and Twitter put up concerted efforts to block false stories of 'miracle cures' and downgrade dubious conspiracy theories in their recommendations. YouTube promised to remove all videos suggesting a relation between 5G wireless technology and the coronavirus. More remarkably, the Dutch government actively fought misinformation using various online strategies. In early April, they started to hire vloggers and popular YouTube influencers, such as YouTuber Rutger Vink ('Furtjuh', 720,000 followers), to promote the coronavirus measures (RTL Nieuws, 2 April, 2020). Later, this strategy backfired when some of these influencers turned their back on health authorities' messages and started to support dubious anti-government groups. In more than one respect, government officials learned from this experience that information is not received the same by different communities and that communicative strategies require constant translation and readjustment.

Legacy media unequivocally pointed to social media networks as perpetrators of the infodemic, while strategically reclaiming their institutional authority as trusted channels. During the first two weeks of the outbreak, Dutch national television broadcast two prime-time television shows titled 'Corona: Facts and Fables' (NOS, 13 March, 2020). The format featured an anchor reading out loud questions sent by viewers and posted on social media; they were answered by medical experts, including RIVM Director Jaap van Dissel, and by national and local policy-makers, such as Minister of Medical Care, Bruno Bruins. Mainstream news media almost unanimously conformed to the crisis response frame, showing how the system got stretched to its limits while experts explained the urgency of the situation. Daily statistics and predictive models dominated the headlines of legacy news media. A majority of news reports between mid-March and mid-April assumed the narrative frame of a 'race against the clock' where the robustness of medical institutions was at risk. Visuals showing ICUs filled with medical equipment, nurses and doctors were alternated with images of coffins and improvised mortuaries from Italy, underscoring predictions of the dire straits the Dutch health system would face if it collapsed.

Interestingly, the images that circulated through social media, while equally urgent, were different in nature. Social media networks appeared the preferred means of medical staff and patients to communicate their feelings and observations; they helped 'experiential witnesses' to act as embedded citizen-journalists and cool-headed reporters from the battle field. For patients in isolation, receiving social media messages and clips from their family and friends provided great comfort, and their self-recorded video messages from the ICU frequently went viral. For medical staff working in the frontlines of corona care—an area off limits to journalists—social media clips helped mediate their emotional narratives about death and suffering. Several doctors and nurses became instant celebrities on YouTube and Facebook, even to the point where 'established' influencers promoted these professionals' self-recorded clips on their channels. Social media also served as 'weapons of mass appreciation' when users rallied support for healthcare workers by staging, recording and distributing spontaneous public applause sessions. This communication style propelled by social media turned out to be immensely popular, leading the public news channel to quickly launch a new daily programme called 'Frontberichten' ('Messages from the front') (NPO2, 20 March, 2020). Its format was a simple 15-minute concatenation of video clips self-recorded by nurses, doctors, ambulance staff and by patients hospitalized in various parts of the country. The programme resembled a televised Facebook news feed—an instance of legacy media borrowing the 'live streaming' strategy preferred by social media.

In sum, the institutional model of health communication clearly reigned the emergency response phase. Expert voices were in the lead; the government sought the exclusive advice of medical and scientific experts; evidence-informed policy-making got distributed by mass media. However, policy-makers and news media effectively countered and co-opted non-expert attacks by deploying its own social media dynamics, thus amplifying their own authority. And even if social media was disturbingly weaponized to sow distrust and propel misinformation, the institutions of government and mass media also adopted the strengths of social media—its distribution power, logic and style—to enhance their authority and gain the public's trust. In other words, the two models of health communication turned out to be less distinct as they appear. Social media appeared as instruments of transmission *and translation*, requiring constant interaction and adjustment between health experts, government officials, mass media and citizens. The power of the networked model as a tool for the constant readjustment of health information became even more poignant when the initial emergency response evolved into the next stage of the public debate: the smart exit strategy.

The 'smart exit strategy' stage

A month after the government imposed a self-described 'intelligent lockdown', the call for a 'smart opening up' started to put pressure on policy-makers who got caught between medical experts recommending to flatten the infection curve and economic experts urging to curb the budget deficit. With the pandemic and the public debate entering this new stage, the monopoly of medical experts on informing policy-makers was increasingly disputed: Who counts as an expert, what counts as proper advice and how should institutional authorities weigh information voiced by a variety of experts and multiple non-experts? Social media took on an increasingly pertinent role in the circulation of knowledge and information during this next stage of the public debate, focusing on developing smart exit strategies.

In early April of 2020, the disputation between those who support a prolonged lockdown and those who favour a less strict regime moved to the centre of public debate. Public policy-making is normally directed by a cost-benefit analysis: achieving maximum societal benefit for the least cost. But at the height of the corona crisis, the public debate pushed a novel twist: How many deaths are we prepared to accept at what economic cost? Popular talk show host Jort Kelder—neither a medical professional nor an economic expert—allegedly voiced the concerns of entrepreneurs and business people when raising the question: How much money do we spend to save the lives of elderly and patients with underlying conditions—including obesity and smoking—whose deaths are immanent anyway (NPO1, 4 April, 2020)? The interview clip went viral and a storm erupted on Twitter, where both sides navigated public opinion. Policy-makers weathered the storm of sentiments by reclaiming institutional authority, asking why self-respecting media invited 'non-expert celebrities' to air uninformed and contested perspectives.

Gradually, government officials became aware of the need to involve nonmedical experts, professionals and non-experts from civil society to shape future exit strategies. In an attempt to open up the small circle of expertise to broader input, Minister of Economic Affairs Eric Wiebes put himself at the helm of an effort to develop the 'one-and-a-half-metre society'—a model for opening up businesses and public life while abiding by the stringent measures for social distancing. Entrepreneurs had started to complain that the economy was now in the 'intensive care' while governmental policy-making continued to be dictated by the 'medical establishment'. Wiebes had to carefully weigh his 'smart opening up' strategy against the still reigning medical emergency response narrative. He asked institutions, including schools, sports clubs and public transport to help engineer solutions to rekindle economic activity; he also invited restaurants, office workers and shop owners to creatively balance off paced customer traffic with economic viability. Individuals and small business enthusiastically sent in their solutions, such as turning underused hotel rooms into office space, while artists and designers offered their help to transform existing spaces.

When Prime Minister Rutte announced, on 21 April, that the smart lockdown had to be prolonged for another month, arguing that the complex practicalities of the one-and-a-half-metre society did not yet align with epidemiologists' recommendations, his announcement was met with resignation and disbelief. Despite the government's attempts to crowdsource technical, medical, economic and social solutions, a mounting choir of critical voices complained that public policy-making was still exclusively primed by an 'expertocracy' of medical authorities. Various commentators started to call for a reassessment of government measures, based on more and broader expert-input; they required more transparency from the government in opening up their arguments for policy choices (NRC Handelsblad, 27 April 2020; NPO2, 25 April, 2020). In order to retain trust, policy-makers felt the heat to gauge public sentiment against scientific rationale, and to weigh experts' limited judgment against strong public appeals to weigh counterarguments and communal emotions.

Two such appeals evolved in May and June. The first concerned media celebrity and opinion poll strategist Maurice de Hond, who launched a public dispute with the RIVM. He reasoned that the proven possibility of airborne (aerosol) transmission as one of the modes of transmission of COVID-19 was cause to dismiss the government's social distancing measure on scientific grounds. Later in

July, the second stage of the pandemics claim was seconded by a group of mostly nonmedical scientists proposing 'emerging evidence' of airborne spread to the WHO, urging the global body to update its guidance on how COVID-19 passes between people. The second group calling into question the government's preferred exit strategy was a grassroots movement called 'Viruswaanzin' ('Virus idiocy'); it was organized by self-proclaimed non-expert Willem Engel whose effort to annul the government's corona policy gained clout through Facebook, YouTube and Twitter. After his video clip went viral, over 500,000 Dutch citizens signed a petition protesting the prolonged enforcement of social distancing measures in all public places. The protesters took their case to court, where the judge dismissed their claim that the government had no legitimate grounds for its one-and-a-half-metre policy and should therefore disband it (Volkskrant, 25 June, 2020). Although different in scope and result, both public appeals called upon ordinary citizens to dispute 'scientific evidence' as the ground for the government's legitimacy to enforce unpopular policies. Both groups framed their struggles as battles for transparency and democracy, deploying the power of social media to enforce checks and balances on government policies.

During the second stage of the pandemic, we saw many more instances of nonexpert voices thrusting forward their claims to provide 'alternative' scientific evidence through social media channels—claims that were subsequently discussed by legacy news media. Scientists and policy-makers were repeatedly challenged to adjust their information strategies; their attempts to appropriate social media logic and dynamics were not always successful and sometimes even backfired. But along the way, they managed to adapt their strategies by translating information to various target groups and through different channels, allowing more types of arguments and rendering the debate between officials and citizens more dialogic. Although the attacks on institutions and institutional expertise never led to a serious decline of trust in their legitimacy in the Netherlands, there is a notable difference between the 'crisis response' stage and the 'smart exit' phase of the public debate involving COVID-19 related health information; we will reflect on this in the last section.

Conclusion

So what does the Dutch public debate on COVID-19 response teach us about health communication as an intricate process of information exchange, public debate and knowledge translation? We can take away at least three important points from our analysis of the two-tiered debate: (1) Social media are deployed to both undermine and enhance public trust in scientific expertise during a health crisis; (2) the networked-translation model of health communication has transformed rather than replaced the institutional-transmission model; and (3) institutional actors engaged in this process need to develop distinct communication strategies at the various stages of a public debate. Since health crises like this corona pandemic are likely to have significant impact on institutional processes of communication in the future, we want to reflect on each of these three insights.

First, it is crucial to acknowledge that social media are indeed two-sided swords of health communication. They facilitate the rampant distribution of misinformation about COVID-19 at the same time and by the same means as they can help officials to spread accurate information about the disease. The strategy of institutions to adopt social media platforms to fight misinformation and to collaborate with platform owners to counter the infodemic, while inevitable, is not without risks. Hiring YouTube influencers to spread government rules about social distancing and other preventive measures may work well one day; the next day, the same influencers may propagate messages that defy the official one, because they are paid by another interested party to do so. It is important to keep in mind that social media platforms are commercial environments serving the marketplace of ideas rather than the common good (Van Dijck et al. 2018; Napoli 2019).

Second, it may be comforting to conclude from the above analysis that the public's trust is still firmly anchored in the expert knowledge of professionals and embedded in authoritative contexts. However, the increasing pressure from social media platforms assuming a central position in the networked distribution of information marks a significant transformation of the institutional model by increasingly including elements of translation. Unsurprisingly, social media platforms are heavily invested in gaining a position of institutional authority themselves. In the midst of the corona crisis, only 21% of all Dutch users trusted social media as reliable news sources, compared to 63% who trust news organizations, even though users receive more than 50% of their news through social media channels (NU.nl, 12 May, 2020). Scientists, policy-makers and professional journalists have come to rely on social media networks to receive and send information, because these platforms allow access to the public debate in various direct ways. For public institutions to become dependent on major online channels, whose technological features and business models are squarely at odds with their own institutional processes, they need to exercise constant scrutiny and keen awareness of the risks and benefits involved in borrowing social media tactics, mechanics and style. Therefore, professional health communicators need to be constantly aware of the affordances of various social media platforms, as well as the differences between user communities.

Third, looking at the two stages of the public debate in the period following the COVID-19 outbreak, we have noticed that the process of health communication during the 'crisis response' phase was different from the 'smart exit' phase, requiring different strategies from institutions in general and from policy-makers in particular. Although there is a fair amount of relevant research about health communication strategies during a time of crisis (Chon and Park 2021; Oh et al. 2020), research on the phase following the emergency is rather scarce. During the 'crisis response' stage, the public debate roughly followed the linear vectors of information projected in the institutional model, assigning authority to scientific experts and government voices. The second phase, however, reflected the capricious flows of the networked model, allowing more space to non-experts and citizens, whose voices, amplified by social media, gained traction in unexpected and inexplicable ways, hence requiring more 'translational skills' from policy-makers and professional communicators. Obviously, they have to learn how to navigate complex new information environments at various stages of the debate; they have to engage with divergent kinds of stakeholders and understand the power of social media as a centrifugal force in communication processes (Duffy 2018).

Looking at the COVID-19 public debate in the Netherlands, we can conclude from our analysis that non-expert voices expressed through social media channels have substantial impact on the translation of health information and the steering of the public debate, particularly when the immediate crisis response yields to a less urgent phase. The transformed nature of health science communication process unmistakably impacts the public's trust in institutions. More comparative and empirical research is needed to investigate how various models of science communication contribute to long-term trust in science and policy-making (Schäfer 2016). Indeed, for scientists, policy-makers and journalists to navigate and control the new reality propelled by a networked-translation model of health communication, it is important to understand how they can refurbish institutional trust to shape information flows in this constantly changing media landscape.

Acknowledgements

The authors received financial support from the Horizon 2020 research project 'Policy, Expertise and Trust in Action (PERITIA)', Grant agreement No. 870883.

Note

1 We collected and analysed official policy documents on government sites (Rijksoverheid.nl), ministry's press conferences, articles from mass media outlets such as television (NOS Nieuws; talkshows from NPO1, NPO2 and NPO3; special COVID-19-related programming on public broadcasting channels and RTL Nieuws) and newspapers and sites (NRC Handelsblad, Volkskrant; NU.nl). Media sources appear in a seperate list below.

References

Secondary sources

Benkler, Y., Faris, R., and Roberts, H. (2018). *Network Propaganda: Manipulation, Disinformation, and Radicalization in American Politics*, New York: Oxford University Press.

Bjørkdahl, K., and Carlsen, B. (2019). 'Enacting pandemics: How health authorities use the press—and vice versa', in K. Bjørkdahl and B. Carlsen (Eds.), *Pandemics, Publics, and Politics*, Singapore: Palgrave Pivot, 43–58.

Botsman, R. (2017). *Who Can You Trust? How Technology Brought Us Together and Why It Could Drive Us Apart*, New York: Penguin.

Bradshaw, S., and Howard, P. (2018). *Challenging Truth and Trust: A Global Inventory of Organized Social Media Manipulation*, Oxford: Oxford Internet Institute.

Chon, M.-G., and Park, H. (2021). 'Predicting public support for government actions in a public health crisis', *Health Communication* 36(4): 476–486.

Crawford, M. B. (2019). 'Algorithmic governance and political legitimacy', *American Affairs* 3(2): 73–94.

Dahlgren, P. (2018). 'Media, knowledge and trust: The deepening epistemic crisis of democracy', *Javnost – The Public* 25(1–2): 20–27.

Davies, W. (2018). *Nervous States: How Feeling Took Over the World*, New York: Vintage.

Duffy, B. (2018). *The Perils of Perception*, London: Atlantic Books.

EU vs DiSiNFO (2020). EEAS Special Report Update: Short assessments of narratives and disinformation aournd the Covid-19 pandemic, https://euvsdisinfo.eu/eeas-special-report-update-short-assessment-of-narratives-and-disinformation-around-the-covid-19-pandemic-update-december-2020-april-2021/

Garrett, L. (2020). 'The art of medicine. COVID-19: The medium is the message', *The Lancet* 395: 942–943.

Hagen, L., Keller, T., Neely, S., DePaula, N., and Robert-Cooperman, C. (2018). 'Crisis communications in the age of social media: A network analysis of Zika-related tweets', *Social Science Computer Review* 36(5): 523–541.

Lazer, D. M., Baum, M. A., Benkler, Y., Berinsky, A. J., Greenhill, K. M., Menczer, F., Metzger, M. J., Nyhan, B., Pennycook, G., Rothchild, D., Schudson, M., Sloman, S. A., Sunstein, C. R., Thorson, E. A., Watts, D. J., and Zittrain, J. L. (2018). 'The science of fake news', *Science* 359(6380): 1094–1096.

Limaye, R. J., Sauer, M., Ali, J., Bernstein, J., Wahl, B., Barnhill, A., and Labrique, A. (2020). 'Building trust while influencing online COVID-19 content in the social media world', *The Lancet* 2(6): E277–E278.

Llewellyn, S. (2020). 'Covid-19: How to be careful with trust and expertise on social media', *British Medical Journal* 368: m1160.

Napoli, P. (2019). *Social Media and the Public Interest: Media Regulation in the Disinformation Age*, New York: Columbia University Press.

Oh, S.-H., Lee, S. Y., and Han, C. (2020). 'The effects of social media use on preventive behaviors during infectious disease outbreaks: The mediating role of self-relevant emotions and public risk perception', *Health Communication* 36(8): 972–981.

Oreskes, N. (2019). *Why Trust Science?*, Ithaca, NY: Princeton University Press.

Pym, A. (2020). 'When trust matters more than translation', *Pursuit* (29 July), https://pursuit.unimelb.edu.au/articles/when-trust-matters-more-than-translation

Rijksoverheid.nl (2020). https://www.rijksoverheid.nl/onderwerpen/coronavirus-covid-19

Schäfer, M. S. (2016). 'Mediated trust in science: concept, measurement and perspectives for the "science of science communication"', *Journal of Science Communication* 15(5): 1–8.

Simon, T., Goldberg, A., and Adini, B. (2015). 'Socializing in emergencies—A review of the use of social media in emergency situations', *International Journal of Information Management* 35(5): 609–619.

Song, C., and Lee, J. (2015). 'Citizens' use of social media in government, perceived transparency, and trust in government', *Public Performance & Management Review* 39: 430–453.

Tufekçi, Z. (2019). 'The internet has made dupes—and cynics—of us all', *Wired* (24 June, 2019), https://www.wired.com/story/internet-made-dupes-cynics-of-us-all/

Van Dijck, J. (1995). *Manufacturing Babies and Public Consent: Debating the New Reproductive Technologies*, New York: New York University Press.

Van Dijck, J., Poell, T., and de Waal, M. (2018). *The Platform Society: Public Values in a Connective World*, New York: Oxford University Press.

Weible, C. M. (2020). 'COVID-19 and the policy sciences: initial reactions and perspectives', *Policy Sciences* 53: 225–241.

Weingart, P., and Joubert, M. (2019). 'The conflation of motives of science communication—causes, consequences, remedies', *Journal of Science Communication* 18(3): 1–13.

Wiederhold, B. K. (2020). 'Using social media to our advantage: Alleviating anxiety during a pandemic', *Cyberpsychology, Behavior & Social Networking* 23(4): 1–2.

Yang, G. (2020). 'Communication as translation: Notes toward a new conceptualization of communication', in M. Powers and A. Russell (Eds.), *Rethinking Media Research for Changing Societies*, Cambridge: Cambridge University Press, 184–194.

Media sources

NOS (13 March, 2020). Coronavirus: Feiten en fabels, https://nos.nl/artikel/2324856-het-coronavirus-feiten-en-fabels-volg-hier-de-extra-nos-uitzending.html

NPO1 (17 March, 2020). Een Vandaag, https://eenvandaag.avrotros.nl/panels/opiniepanel/alle-uitslagen/item/groot-vertrouwen-in-rutte-en-zijn-aanpak-van-het-coronavirus-na-toespraak/

NPO1 (4 April, 2020). Op1, https://www.uitzendinggemist.net/zenders/Nederland-1.html

NPO2 (20 March, 2020). Frontberichten, https://www.bnnvara.nl/frontberichten/jouwfrontberichtinsturen

NPO2 (25 April, 2020). Nieuwsuur, https://nos.nl/nieuwsuur/artikel/2331727-wetenschappers-bekritiseren-gebrek-aan-openheid-corona-adviezen.html

NRC Handelsblad (27 April, 2020). https://www.nrc.nl/nieuws/2020/04/27/overheid-wees-transparant-in-strijd-tegen-het-coronavirus-a3997982

NU.nl (17 March, 2020). https://www.nu.nl/tech/6038048/techbedrijven-vs-pakken-samen-desinformatie-over-coronavirus-aan.html

NU.nl (12 May, 2020). https://www.nu.nl/media/5882901/meerderheid-nieuwsconsumenten-wantrouwt-sociale-media-als-nieuwsbron.html

RTL Nieuws (2 April, 2020). https://www.rtlnieuws.nl/nieuws/politiek/artikel/5078491/influencers-gaan-opdracht-over-overheid-jongeren-overtuigen

Volkskrant (25 June, 2020). https://www.volkskrant.nl/nieuws-achtergrond/in-de-rechtbank-stoort-viruswaanzin-zich-eerst-aan-het-spatscherm-en-dan-aan-de-rechter~bdff8b1e/

3 Trust and Cooperation through Social Media

COVID-19 translations for Chinese communities in Melbourne

Anthony Pym and Bei Hu

How might a pandemic change research on translation?

Researchers working on language and culture have broadly adopted a 'post-truth' epistemology. Critical discourse analysis, narrative analysis, deconstruction and the like all fight good fights, showing complexity where others see simple oppositions, opening awareness to wider pluralities and more inclusive narratives and promulgating critical thought. Truth, at least on the level of any causation beyond language, is no longer the battleground that matters. It is enough for intellectuals to question trust, to encourage diversity and dissent from the official. In a world of pandemics, vaccinations and a climate emergency, however, a certain kind of truth enacts revenge, albeit not as any exact representation. Dissent, difference and distrust lead to people dying and planetary perdition. Research on language and culture cannot be business as usual—cheap puns and professional subversion are no longer enough.

One way of addressing this epistemological challenge is through the notion of performative simulacra (after Baudrillard 1981). Just as the person who pretends to be ill can actually become ill as a result, so simulacra can *perform* the thing that is represented, becoming an action that is more than a mere representation and can thus lead to action. This can be seen in a simple model of behaviour-change communication: the spread of a virus and the warming of the planet are represented by numbers (deaths, degrees of temperature); those data are represented by the models of science; those models and their conclusions in turn underlie the simulacra of science that appear in public policy. From there, further chains of simulacra work through various media in order to reach people whose behaviour might be changed as a result. In multilingual societies such as Melbourne,

DOI: 10.4324/9781003183907-4

Australia, where more than 260 languages are spoken at home, multiple translations and retellings enter the picture as simulacra as well, ideally performing in such a way as to achieve non-coercive behaviour change in the many culturally and linguistically diverse (CALD) communities. The interest of this model is that, at every stage in the chain of representations, the receivers have to *trust* the simulacra in order for the representations to perform—there is no requirement and often little expectation for full understanding of any anterior truth; it is enough that the simulacra are believed in as speaking for the distant and otherwise unintelligible nature, as did the gods in another age. And this trust in the simulacrum is especially acute in the steps that involve translation across languages and cultures, since it is in those particular passages that we find fewer shared referents, less familiarity, a wider range of expectations and consequently greater risks of disbelief, denial and dissent. Distrust can undo the simulacra at every step along the way, but distrust of translations is a particularly corrosive solvent. The special relation between translation and trust is thus a question of degree rather than nature, which means that lessons can be learned from the way other kinds of simulacra perform.

Our aim here is to study the degrees of trust and distrust in translations (including spoken translations and retellings) in COVID-19 communication in Melbourne, Victoria, in 2020.

Behaviour-change communication

Information flows concerning a pandemic are not just any old health-care communication. They are not focused on doctor–patient interactions: their prime aim is to change collective behaviour on a wide scale.

That aim is quite different from health literacy, understood as 'accurate health information and services that people can easily find, understand and use to inform their decisions and actions' (Department of Health and Human Services 2020: n.p.): Tell me about the different ways to treat or not to treat my cancer, and then let me decide. A society's level of health literacy can be measured and improved. For example, in the Australian state of Victoria it was found that 43% of the Australian-born population had basic health literacy, while the figure was only 26% for people whose first language was not English (Ethnic Communities' Council of Victoria [ECCV] 2012: 12). A recent report (ECCV 2020: 4) suggests that, while there might have been 'a small improvement' in health literacy overall, it remains unsatisfactory in the growing linguistically diverse communities, where dedicated outreach is needed. But that is literacy.

Behaviour-change communication, unlike literacy enhancement, is not limited to informing an individual decision on the part of the recipient: it aims to change collective behaviour for the general good, since successful outcomes depend on everyone adopting the new behaviour. In the case of a pandemic, this is clear enough: wearing a mask, respecting social distancing and so on only work if everyone adopts those measures, since the chains of cause-and-effect concern more than one human body and thus more than one individual's decision. The same logic might be applied to climate-emergency discourse, where the change in behaviour has to be general and must extend beyond cultures and national borders if it is to prolong the viability of human economies.

Trust in science

Behaviour-change communication thus differs fundamentally from an evidence-based presentation of data or risk calculations. It is not enough that the receiver of communication presumes to understand the findings of science or to comprehend the hazards—in most cases these days we are well beyond the point where citizens expect to fully comprehend the discourses of experts. This means that, in addition to not misleading the end-user, behaviour-change communication requires that messages be trusted to special degrees.

The *Edelman Trust Barometer* (2021) shows that trust in all information sources reached record lows during the pandemic in 2020. A search for trust might thus explain why evidence-based strategies were sidelined in some governments' COVID-19 communication. A prime example is the New Zealand government, which was considered successful in terms of the communicative aspects of crisis management (Cousins 2020; McGuire et al. 2020). Examination of the shifts in tone and the multifaceted crisis communications used by Prime Minister Jacinda Ardern shows that her initial evidence-based discourse moved towards a more empathetic approach, aimed at encouraging solidarity. In times of crisis, 'a care ethics approach' (McGuire et al. 2020: 365) can forge trust and goodwill between leader and public.

Trust is a peculiar object of knowledge in this regard. For us, trust is primarily interpersonal: we trust a message because of the sender as configured by the medium, and only then in terms of whether the content makes sense to us. This kind of trust entails an element of risk (Luhmann 1988: 103): since we cannot understand the science directly, we cannot know whether the people we trust actually understand it or they are setting out to mislead or betray us.

This uncertainty risk factor distinguishes trust from predictability. Further, trust typically emerges from the confluence of many different factors, feeding into intuitions and emotional responses that lie beyond the range of what we can readily analyse, whereas distrust is often attributable to just one factor or event that has a cataclysmic effect on all others. It is methodologically much easier to say how trust is lost than how it is gained.

Trust of this kind is of particular interest for the study of translational simulacra. If we choose to act on the basis of something that comes from a language and a culture we are not familiar with, risk-based trust is always involved.

In the following sections, the ways in which trust can be built, maintained and broken are illustrated through four case studies of how COVID-19 information was received in a context of post-truth simulacra. We are especially interested in the role played by social media.

Study 1: Trust in media at the national level

To identify how trust works in relation to translations and social media, we first turn to a useful background study that, remarkably and lamentably, does not look at translations. In April 2020, Park et al. (2020) conducted an online survey of 2,196 Australians aged 18 or older to explore how this controlled and weighted sample received and trusted COVID-19 information. Special attention was paid to the factors that might affect people's trust in news coverage during a pandemic accompanied by an infodemic (World Health Organization 2020). The survey did not, however, look at any language variables: it assumed that all participants spoke English to the same degree. As such, it serves us here as a baseline from which to measure the importance of languages other than English.

Not surprisingly, more Australians were accessing news more than once a day (70% in 2020, up from 56% in 2019). Some 92% said they were either extremely or somewhat concerned about COVID-19. The study also found that anxiety was being compounded by the increased volumes of COVID-19 information.

With regard to information sources, traditional news media (print and television) were the most common way to receive COVID-19 information (61%), followed by social media (38%), department of health websites (32%) and state government websites (28%). Other sources included personal communication (25%), 'experts' (20%), politicians (19%) and the WHO website (10%). In terms of information channels, television (51%) was the most popular medium for COVID-19 information, followed by online news (27%), social media (21%), radio (7%) and print (6%).

There are clear generational differences in the types of information channels people relied on. Those aged 18–22 used social media the most to gain news about COVID-19 (68%), compared with 21% of those aged 55–73 and 10% of those aged 74 or more. Facebook was the most popular social platform for COVID-related information (49%). Other surveyed platforms included YouTube (21%), Google News (21%), Instagram (14%), Facebook Messenger (14%), WhatsApp (10%) and Twitter (10%). All these platforms are owned by American companies and the majority of users are assumed to be English speakers. The media landscape might be different if other language communities are considered.

The younger generations are clearly the major consumers of social media, while older generations are found to rely more on traditional news media. This is no surprise. Yet it can have consequences for the way different media are trusted. Park et al. (2020: 28) report that the younger generations actively checked information from government or health authority websites more often than did the older generations. Social media are thus associated with a verification function. This is of interest to us because, when receivers regularly check information across media, the result can be a decrease in trust in official messages. As is well known, social media can entail an 'echo chamber' effect that enables trust to be limited to like-minded users. This leads to more polarized groups who mainly share and trust the information that adheres to their own belief systems (Del Vicario et al. 2016; Allcott and Gentzkow 2017: 211; Sunstein 2001; Pariser 2011).

Park et al. (2020: 24) did not find a linear relationship between trust and preferred source of information. Overall, the respondents deemed 'experts' to be the most credible source of COVID-19 information (85% 'agree'), followed by health organizations (78%), state and federal governments (67% and 66%, respectively) and news organizations (61%). Only 21% of the respondents agreed that social media were trustworthy, the lowest score of all, even though 38% of all respondents reported using those same media. Not everyone who uses social media believes in them. At the other end of the scale, 'experts' were the most trusted source of information but only 20% of the respondents reported having accessed them. People believe experts, but not many use them.

It is not hard to make sense of this apparent paradox. On the one hand, although there was concern about the spread of false news about COVID-19, a clear majority (77%) of the participants reported that they had not come across excessive misinformation. Two-thirds of those who had seen misinformation reported encountering it on social media, whereas health authorities and 'experts' were the least-cited sources.

Park et al. (2020) thus find a certain relation between social media and trust in a monolingual context: 'experts', governments and traditional media are generally trusted, whereas social media are generally less trusted. The study also clearly indicates that the main users of social media, the younger generations, are also the groups with access to the widest range of information sources. Younger users are thus more given to checking information and comparing sources.

Study 2: Trust in media in a week of lockdown

We now zoom in to a particular case study where different media were used in an emergency situation in a multilingual context. On 4 July 2020, active COVID cases were detected in a group of nine inner-Melbourne public-housing towers. About 3,000 residents were suddenly ordered not to leave their homes and were constrained from doing so.

What happened in the following week later became the object of an extensive report by the Victorian Ombudsman (2020). The report brings together submissions from many parties, offering a view from the 'inside'—the end-users of information. It also makes several points concerning languages, since some 30% of the residents had previously registered as preferring to receive information in languages other than English. The affected population actually spoke some seven community languages as well as English, and translations were reportedly provided in all those languages. The nature of the communication, however, depended very much on the medium employed:

Formal printed letters

'Owing to translation and distribution delays, written materials explaining the Detention Directions in community languages were not distributed to households until the fifth and sixth days of the intervention—in the latter case, the same day the directions were revoked' (Victorian Ombudsman 2020: 15). Although formal letters were legally necessary, the time delays meant they did little to help residents understand what was happening. As simulacra, they merely performed authority.

Websites

A Department of Health website included a guide on how to make complaints. The guide was available in Easy English and more than 20 community languages. 'However, the guide did not include specific information about making complaints about the exercise of powers by Authorised Officers, did not identify what methods had been approved by the Secretary for making such complaints, if any, [and] was not distributed to residents at 33 Alfred Street during the lockdown' (Victorian Ombudsman 2020: 98). So even the best translated website is potentially ineffectual if it does not include practical information and if people do not know where it is. One of the residents commented, 'I think honestly it was only [when a community advocate] posted it [information about making a complaint] on the WhatsApp group that we made a complaint to the Ombudsman' (Victorian Ombudsman 2020: 98). The simulacrum is ineffectual if it cannot be found.

Public announcements

Submissions from one resident indicate that information was broadcast over a public-address system: 'There was only one announcement of the lockdown [...] and it was in English'. The resident said a further announcement was Arabic: '[It said] something like, "the lockdown is continuing and there are another nine days to go" [...] It wasn't very clear' (Victorian Ombudsman 2020: 86). People lose trust when they feel neglected.

Professional interpreters

Qualified interpreters were present in the initial stages of the lockdown but not in sufficient numbers or enough languages for messages to be trusted: 'There was [...] *an unacceptable absence of qualified interpreters* at the Flemington and North Melbourne public housing estates during the critical first evening of the lockdown, leaving residents from non-English speaking backgrounds to rely upon the assistance of neighbours, family members and community advocates to understand the circumstances under which they were being detained' (Victorian Ombudsman 2020: 17; emphasis added). Again, one cannot trust what is not there.

Word of mouth

The role of 'neighbours, family members and community advocates' is noted as filling in the gap left by the insufficient presence of interpreters. In another part of the report we find specific mention of younger family members, who have presumably learned English at school in Australia: 'Residents and advocates observed that owing to [an] initial lack of official information in community languages, it primarily fell upon *younger, English-speaking family members and community volunteers* to explain details of the lockdown to non-English-speaking residents' (Victorian Ombudsman 2020: 153; emphasis added).

Electronic messaging

Several comments point to the importance of electronic messaging of various kinds as an extension of word of mouth, especially when face-to-face communication became limited and risky. Perhaps paradoxically, a submission from Translators and Interpreters Australia, a union organization, mentions this: 'Organisations working at the frontline undertook to develop their own immediate audio and SMS messages. Several days into the crisis, grassroots initiatives were filling gaps that should have been government responsibility' (Victorian Ombudsman 2020: 153). And in the report itself: 'Perceived shortcomings in information provided by DHHS [Department of Health and Human Services] also saw some community organisations produce and distribute their own materials explaining the lockdown for multicultural communities' (Victorian Ombudsman 2020: 153).

In all, the report shows that the more traditional media had significant shortcomings with respect to translated information: print was too slow, the public-address system was not well understood, websites were at best useful for those who could find them in English, and professional interpreters were difficult to engage on very short notice. These shortcomings created communication gaps that were then filled by word of mouth, SMS messaging and the electronic transfer of voice messages, where translation and less formal modes of translanguaging were more likely to occur on an ad hoc basis. According to the report, these latter media were used by non-official, non-professional mediators, variously described as 'community advocates', 'community volunteers' and organizations that were 'grassroots' and 'frontline'.

Some of these mediators elsewhere confirmed the Ombudsman report. Li Guangneng, a community leader in the East Timor-Chinese community, told ABC Chinese News (Fang 2020) that the residents barely knew about the government's lockdown plan, let alone other information on the pandemic. Similarly, we independently learned from the Chinese Community Social Services Centre (CCSSC) that an elderly Chinese-speaking couple who resided in public housing in North Melbourne did not leave their apartment for weeks because they thought their building was on the lockdown list. Not until social workers called did they realize they were not in one of the nine towers concerned. When asked why the elderly couple could not obtain information through regular information channels, one social worker said, 'I don't think they have any information sources at all. They had no idea what was going on' (see a detailed analysis of this and similar cases in Karidakis et al. 2022).

When we now consider the distribution of trust across the various media, it seems that an 'us' vs. 'them' opposition was in operation. As far as the residents were concerned, messages from print, websites and qualified interpreters came from the official 'them', whereas messages via word of mouth and electronic media were from senders closer to 'us' and were more likely to be in the residents' language. SBS News (Wu 2020) reported the case of an elderly man living in one of the locked-down towers who said that because one of the COVID-19 testing staff could speak Chinese, he felt much less anxious and trusted the government's strategy. The power of authority alone might not build trust in 'them'—there was little trust in any of the official media in this case. Linguistic and cultural mediation, however, seems to have been more able to create trust by bridging the gap between 'them' and 'us'.

In this case study, the official communication was so haphazard that it led to enhanced distrust. The Ombudsman reports: 'Several residents who spoke with investigators said the lockdown had resulted in significant distrust of [the Department of Health] and other public authorities'. In the words of one resident, 'How could you trust someone like that after what they had just done to us in the last two weeks?' (Victorian Ombudsman 2020: 163).

When we look at the monolingual baseline studied by Park et al. (2020), the most trusted media in Australia are health authorities, 'experts' and television, with social media at the bottom of the bucket. In the housing-estate lockdown, though, that distribution seems to have been reversed: official media were held in suspicion, while social media were turned to for messages that could be better understood and trusted. We suspect that part of the discrepancy ensues from the reductive method adopted by Park et al. (2020), who assumed receivers were culturally and linguistically homogenous. Move beyond that assumption, and the different simulacra become more dynamic.

Following the housing lockdown and a series of heavily publicized language-management errors, the Victorian Government set up a task force to look into the communication problems encountered. One of the main take-aways from the Ombudsman report was that they had been using the wrong media: they had to devote far more attention to WhatsApp as a medium for most language communities and to WeChat for Chinese (Victorian Government 2020).

Study 3: Trust in community mediation

As noted, Park et al. (2020) find that younger people are both prone to use social media and likely to check one source against another, incorporating an element of distrust into their reception process. So what happens when media users are not young? This question was particularly important in the COVID-19 pandemic, where the elderly were the most at risk of dying.

Almost one in three Australians aged 50 or over were born in non-English-speaking countries (FECCA 2015). In Melbourne, the percentage of people aged over 65 with low English language proficiency may be as high as 76% among Mandarin speakers (Department of Immigration and Border Protection 2014). This means that the elderly are particularly dependent on linguistic mediation of various kinds.

As part of a wider study on Melbourne's COVID-19 communications with CALD communities (reported in Karidakis et al. 2022), we carried out focus-group interviews with representatives of the CCSSC, which is the largest social organization for the Chinese elderly in Victoria, and the Australian Chinese Charity Foundation (ACCF). We were particularly interested in how they made pandemic-related information available to the elderly. This is actually how we learned about the above case of the elderly couple who thought they were in hard lockdown for weeks because they had no effective communication to the contrary.

Both organizations stressed that they translated and otherwise conveyed only the official information received from the government, even when they themselves might not always personally agree. This initial trust in government was repeated so often as to be intriguing: it might logically be motivated by the funds that both organizations receive from the government. At the same time, though, there were frequent cases where the elderly reportedly did not understand straight translations of the official messages and required further explanations or turned to additional sources of information. The community organizations thus largely saw their role as being to take the official message and make it trustworthy for the elderly. Although a study focused on younger and newer members of Melbourne's Asian communities found that their respondents 'did not seem to trust their co-ethnic communities as much as they do sources on social media or news sites' (Shin and Song 2021), our interviewees indicated that this did not apply to older members of the same communities.

All the organizations in our wider study reported the need to use a range of media. In the Greek and Italian communities, this involved phone calls to explain issues to the elderly and even printed leaflets to have them believe the message was official. Both the Chinese organizations, however, reported using WeChat as their prime means of communication: 'We do have a website and a Facebook page, but not very frequently updated because our clients barely read it' (CCSSC); 'We do upload certain stuff onto [our] website, but the trend is to go to WeChat chat groups more often than not' (ACCF). The community organizations thus gained the trust of their members through a very particular kind of social media.

Study 4: Trust in WeChat

So how do trust and distrust operate in WeChat, the apparently inescapable information source for the Chinese diaspora?

The Chinese-owned WeChat application has become the most popular social media platform for Chinese users (Iqbal 2020). Since its inception in 2011 as a simple message-exchanging tool, WeChat has become a global social network. By 2020, it hosted over 1.2 billion active monthly users from a wide range of age groups both within and outside China (Statista 2020). The large number of overseas WeChat users has given rise to debates about national-security threats outside of China (see, for example, Ryan et al. 2020), but this seems not to be an issue for the users themselves.

In our investigation of COVID-19 communication in WeChat public accounts in 2020, we found three communication strategies being used to build trust within the Chinese community in Australia.

The first was to provide timely local news, addressing the community in their first language. This is one sense in which translation seemed to fill a gap left by inaccessible information from government. WeChat outlets were trusted not because they were social media, but because traditional media coverage (e.g. newspaper and TV) in Chinese was neither timely nor adequate. When only a few Australia-focused stories are featured on Chinese state-run news agencies, turning to WeChat outlets like *Living in Melbourne* (墨尔本生活资讯) and *WeSydney* (微悉尼) is a coherent choice.

The second strategy used by Chinese-speaking WeChat outlets was to translate information directly from Australian government and mainstream media, usually enhancing it with Chinese memes. For instance, on 9 July 2020 *Melbourne Today* (今日墨尔本) ran a WeChat story about an announcement by Roger Cook, the then Health Minister of Western Australia. The minister's picture was immediately followed by a cute kitten meme with associated responses from the audience, making the message visually Chinese.

Most of these pieces explicitly indicated that their information was based on Australian official sources. Screenshots of Australian departmental media and ministerial logos, mainstream media headlines in English and news images were used as visual means of fostering credibility. The images told readers that the information had been translated from authoritative English sources, thus allowing the Chinese-language WeChat text to appropriate the credibility capital of the source. In fact, fake news, if defined as 'intentionally and verifiably false' (Allcott and Gentzkow 2017: 213), was rare in the WeChat COVID-19 related articles. Even when straight translations were enhanced with Chinese images and references, adapting the message to the community, the WeChat outlets did not attempt to perform a citizens' media function by challenging professional news. Instead, they sought to build trust with their target readers by providing translations based on English-language institutional authorities.

A third strategy by which WeChat outlets won a certain trust from its target readers would appear to contradict this borrowed credibility: there was a tendency to reflect disillusionment with the West, particularly by comparing the Western system with China. This dichotomy was by no means new within the diasporic communities but was intensified by the pandemic. Chinese-speaking online users in particular compared policies and measures implemented in China with those in Australia. WeChat outlets thus provided a space for them to express their cultural belonging.

For instance, following a translated article called 'Why should Melbourne apologize? We're just unlucky!',[1] 17 of the 49 top comments compare Australia with China. In fact, four of the top five comments mention China's COVID-19 measures explicitly, with only one supporting the political leadership of Victoria. What is also noteworthy here is that this article gave rise to online discussion where many readers also showed sympathy for the Australian government.

For instance, the comments with the highest and the fifth highest 'likes' both pointed out that, despite China's strict healthcare measures, Beijing was at that time also experiencing a small-scale outbreak of coronavirus. Here, the receivers proactively engaged with healthcare communication by producing new data and proposing new arguments. In that sense, this kind of translated journalistic text helped shape the formation of a hybridized cultural identity and prompted active communication.

As noted in the context of the public-housing lockdown, social media allow direct dialogue that can form an 'us', opposed to a relatively absent 'them'. In WeChat we nevertheless find some comments that use 'you' to refer to the government. For example: 'Although I am in Victoria, I still want to ask, when you fiercely attacked China, why didn't you realize that China was also the victim of the pandemic? Chinese people are treated unfairly!' (our translation). Of course, this attempt at dialogue is thwarted by the fact that the message is in untranslated Chinese. Regarding the same article, from a different perspective, another reader commented: 'The Victorian premier, we will support you as always. [We've] got your back. You are the best!' (our translation). That too remains untranslated, keeping the dialogue within the diasporic community.

Rather than simply providing COVID-19 information, WeChat articles carry ideological implications that resonate with a large audience in the diasporic community. They effectively operate in a third cultural space that participants can find neither in Australia's mainstream media nor in the Chinese state media. The communication is frequently emotive and ongoing, with people arguing, sometimes fiercely, without consensus.

Conclusion for translation studies

We have seen a background scenario in which, *grosso modo*, an ostensibly monolingual adult populace trusts science and government more than social media. In a sudden lockdown scenario in a multilingual setting, however, speakers of community languages adopt the opposite behaviour: official media are less trusted and social media are more trusted, thanks to a logic of 'us' in the cultural minority community against 'them' in power. And then, specifically in the Chinese-speaking community, we find WeChat forming an intercultural space exceptionally shared by many age groups, not as a medium that is trustworthy in itself but as a forum for discussion and involvement, where individual sense can be made from collective exchanges.

In all these situations, professionally produced translations play a remarkably minor role. Park et al. (2020) make no mention of translation; the lockdown report mentions only the *delays* caused by translations and the relative absence of interpreters; the Chinese community organizations explain that their elderly members struggle to understand officially translated messages (Karidakis et al. 2022). So why were certified translators and interpreters apparently not playing a more prominent role?

During our research in 2020, public concerns over translation were spurred on by two instances where printed materials had mixed languages: Farsi and Urdu in one case (Dalzell 2020), Turkish and Indonesian in the other (Renaldi and Fang 2020). These became memes that ricocheted through both mainstream and social media—very probably the most that the Australian public had ever heard about translation. Print and radio journalists then sought the opinions of academics, including us. And here we faced a dilemma. Do we complain about the deficient translations, as critical theorists should, and thereby further erode public trust in professional translators? Or do we point out, using whatever simulacra of truth we have at hand, that all government translators are officially certified in Australia, that the errors were actually in project management (the translations were not tested) rather than language work, and any translation errors we had detected as academics were relatively minor and without traceable consequences? More pointedly, do we deploy our own science in the hope of winning and extending trust, or do we comment from the sidelines, spinning theoretical pronouncements and a few subversive puns, as might smart intellectuals who are never actually involved?

In that situation, we chose to defend the certified translators, mainly on the basis of empirical evidence gathered through classroom activities (for example, in Pym 2020). But to little avail. As Luhmann (2000) observed, the mass media distinguish between information and noninformation in terms of their own criteria, not in accordance with external truthfulness or long-term ethical functions. The journalists insisted on the scandal, editing our statements on translation to suit their purposes. And then, in response to the press reports, the Victorian government allocated an additional funding of A\$14.3 million for 'locally developed solutions' to healthcare communication (Razin 2020). Of that sum, only A\$2 million was for translation and interpreting services, with the rest going, astutely in our opinion, to 'locally developed solutions'.

If our ethical dilemma was between supporting translators and magnifying errors, the magnification definitely won. There was no substantial truth to it, but it worked nevertheless, as a performative simulacrum. Any scholarly care to enhance public trust was shown to be relatively ineffectual—as Baudrillard (1981) would note, in post-modernity there is no referent, only degrees and kinds of simulacra, where astute journalists on electronic media hold more sway than old school scholars used to the printed word.

So what were those local solutions? In a major policy change, much of that funding went to community organizations such as those that are able to channel messages via WeChat for Chinese and WhatsApp for the other languages. A short government guide called *Best Practice Guide for Translating Content* (2020) includes the following among its recommendations:

- Write in Plain English and keep your sentences short [...] Complex and detailed information risk inaccuracies and are more expensive.
- Ensure you include social media posts in your translated content.
- Fish where the fish are. Don't expect your target audience to come to you.
- Provide information with both visuals and texts.
- Use a trusted, credible source to promote your message [...] For example:
  - Health professionals as a source for information or advice about health issues
  - A local elder as a messenger when reaching out to specific CALD community.

(Victorian Government 2020: 2)

We cite these principles not just for their relative enlightenment but also because, in a document ostensibly about 'translating content', none of these items strictly concerns translation in the narrow sense of linguistic transfer. They have far more to do with the creation of performative simulacra: how to write a text, how to join language and image, how to select media and how to gain and maintain trust through mediators who are not necessarily professional translators.

The government investment and rethinking might indeed have helped create more trust among CALD communities. After 111 days of hard lockdown, the state of Victoria eradicated community trans-missions of COVID. Social cooperation worked, saving many lives. And that non-metaphorical survival constitutes a new truth that belies postmodern simulacra.

Note

1 https://mp.weixin.qq.com/s/uOKaYCnbhSodhOaWG1xhnA

References

Allcott, H., and Gentzkow, M. (2017). 'Social media and fake news in the 2016 election', *Journal of Economic Perspectives* 31(2): 211–236.

Baudrillard, J. (1981). *Simulacres et simulation*, Paris: Galilée.

Cousins, S. (2020). 'New Zealand eliminates COVID-19', *The Lancet* 395(10235): 1474.

Dalzell, S. (2020). 'Government Coronavirus messages left "nonsensical" after being translated into other languages', *ABC News* (13 August), https://www.abc.net.au/news/2020-08-13/coronavirus-messages-translated-to-nonsense-in-other-languages/12550520

Del Vicario, M., Vivaldo, G., Bessi, A., Zollo, F., Scala, A., Caldarelli, G., and Quattrociocchi, W. (2016). 'Echo chambers: Emotional contagion and group polarization on Facebook', *Scientific Reports* 6: 37825.

Department of Health and Human Services (2020). 'History of health literacy definitions', https://health.gov/our-work/healthy-people/healthy-people-2030/health-literacy-healthy-people-2030/history-health-literacy-definitions

Department of Immigration and Border Protection (2014). *The people of Victoria: Statistics from the 2011 Census*, Canberra: Department of Immigration and Border Protection.

Edelman (2021). *Edelman Trust Barometer 2021*, https://www.edelman.com/sites/g/files/aatuss191/files/2021-03/2021%20Edelman%20Trust%20Barometer.pdf

Ethnic Communities' Council of Victoria [ECCV] (2012). *An Investment Not an Expense: Enhancing Health Literacy in Culturally and Linguistically Diverse Communities*, Carlton, Victoria: Ethnic Communities' Council of Victoria.

Ethnic Communities' Council of Victoria [ECCV] (2020). *Communicating about COVID-19: Health Literacy and Languages Services during the Pandemic*, Carlton, Victoria: Ethnic Communities' Council of Victoria.

Fang, J. (2020). '"信息不通", 被封锁下的墨尔本公屋大楼里的华人', *ABC Chinese News* (6 July), https://www.abc.net.au/chinese/2020-07-06/public-housing-estate-under-hard-lockdown/12427322

FECCA (2015). *Review of Australian Research on Older People from Culturally and Linguistically Diverse Backgrounds*, Deakin, ACT: Federation of Ethnic Communities' Councils of Australia.

Iqbal, M. (2020). 'WeChat revenue and usage statistics', https://www.businessofapps.com/data/wechat-statistics/

Karidakis, M., Woodward-Kron, R., Amorati, R., Hu, B., Pym, A., and Hajek, J. (2022). Enhancing COVID-19 public health communication for culturally and linguistically diverse communities: An Australian interview study with community representatives, *Qualitative Heath Communication*, 1(1): 4–26.

Luhmann, N. (1988). 'Familiarity, confidence, trust: Problems and alternatives', in D. Gambetta (Ed.), *Trust: Making and Breaking Cooperative Relations*, Oxford and Cambridge, MA: Basil Blackwell, 94–108.

Luhmann, N. (2000). *The Reality of the Mass Media*, trans. K. Cross, Palo Alto, CA: Stanford University Press.

McGuire, D., Cunningham, J. E. A., Reynolds, K., and Matthews-Smith, G. (2020). 'Beating the virus: An examination of the crisis communication approach taken by New Zealand Prime Minister Jacinda Ardern during the COVID-19 pandemic', *Human Resource Development International* 23(4): 361–379.

Pariser, E. (2011). *The Filter Bubble: What the Internet Is Hiding from You*, London: Penguin.

Park, S., Fisher, C., Lee, J. Y., and McGuinness, K. (2020). *COVID-19: Australian News and Misinformation*, Canberra: University of Canberra News & Media Research Centre.

Pym, A. (2020). 'When trust matters more than translation', *Pursuit* (29 July), https://pursuit.unimelb.edu.au/articles/when-trust-matters-more-than-translation

Razin, N. (2020). 'Victoria to spend $14 million on more multicultural coronavirus support after translation bungles', *SBS News* (13 August), https://www.sbs.com.au/news/victoria-to-spend-14-million-on-more-multicultural-coronavirus-support-after-translation-bungles

Renaldi, E., and Fang, J. (2020). 'Victoria's coronavirus information mistranslated and outdated for migrant communities', *ABC News* (27 October), https://www.abc.net.au/news/2020-10-27/victoria-migrants-concerned-covid-19-information/12815164

Ryan, F., Fritz, A., and Impiombato, D. (2020). *TikTok and WeChat: Curating and Controlling Global Information Flows* (Policy brief), Canberra: Australian Strategic Policy Institute, https://s3-ap-southeast-2.amazonaws.com/ad-aspi/2020-09/TikTok%20and%20WeChat.pdf?VersionId=7BNJWaoHImPVE.6KKcBP1JRD5fRnAVTZ

Shin, W., and Song, J. (2021). 'What our survey fund about effective COVID-19 communications in Asian Australian communities', *Melbourne Asia Review* 5 (12 January), https://melbourneasiareview.edu.au/what-our-survey-found-about-effective-covid-19-communications-in-asian-australian-communities/

Statistia (2020). 'Number of monthly active WeChat users from 2nd quarter 2011 to 3rd quarter 2020', https://www.statista.com/statistics/255778/number-of-active-wechat-messenger-accounts/

Sunstein, C. R. (2001). *Echo Chambers: Bush v. Gore, Impeachment, and Beyond*, Princeton, NJ: Princeton University Press.

Victorian Government (2020). *Best Practice Guide for Translating Content*, https://www.vic.gov.au/interpreters-and-translation-guides

Victorian Ombudsman (2020). *Investigation into the Detention and Treatment of Public Housing Residents Arising from a COVID-19 'Hard Lockdown' in*

July 2020, https://www.ombudsman.vic.gov.au/our-impact/investigation-reports/investigation-into-the-detention-and-treatment-of-public-housing-residents-arising-from-a-covid-19-hard-lockdown-in-july-2020

World Health Organization (2020). '1st WHO Infodemiology Conference', World Health Organization, https://www.who.int/news-room/events/detail/2020/06/30/default-calendar/1st-who-infodemiology-conference

Wu, Y. (2020). '被锁墨市公寓楼的华人，你们好吗?', *SBS Chinese News* (8 July), https://www.sbs.com.au/chinese/mandarin/zh-hans/audio/melbourne-public-housing-chinese-residents-get-support-from-the-community

4 Parallel Pandemic Spaces

Translation, trust and social media

Sharon O'Brien, Patrick Cadwell, and Tetyana Lokot

Introduction

The role of translation (and interpreting) in crisis, emergency or disaster settings has garnered increasing attention over the past few years, even prior to the current COVID-19 pandemic (e.g. Federici 2016; Federici and O'Brien 2020; O'Brien and Federici 2020; Cadwell 2020; O'Mathúna and Hunt 2020; Leeson 2020; Tesseur 2020). The emerging scholarship on the topic of translation in crisis settings illustrates a growing interest in the area as well as the breadth of topics that need to be considered. While there is a growing field of scholarly work on the intertwining of social media and translation on the one hand, and on the role of translation in crisis settings on the other, specific efforts on social media and crisis communication tend to have a blind spot with regard to the role of translation and translator (professional or volunteer) in disseminating information (whether accurately or not) and, ultimately, in dictating behaviour and outcomes in crises such as the global COVID-19 pandemic.

Desjardins (2017) makes a strong case for the study of online social media (OSM) *and* translation by stating that the increased use of OSM has an impact on aspects of human communication and, therefore by extension, on translation. This impact touches specifically on how translators translate, the type of content they translate and the languages being translated (4). Drawing on Standage (2013), she remarks that there is nothing novel about social media but rather the medium on which it takes place and the speed at which communication now occurs are novel (Desjardins 2017: 14). As we shall see, these points are highly relevant for translation in crisis communication via social media, that is speed, the endless communicative loop, and the symbiotic exchange are especially significant for crisis settings.

DOI: 10.4324/9781003183907-5

As stated above, the work done to date on social media and translation for crisis settings specifically is relatively limited. Desjardins (2017) lists 'Translation, Crisis Management and OSM' as one area of study that scholars have given attention to, in particular on the use of web technologies and OSM for the dissemination of communication in disasters and humanitarian response settings. Sutherlin (2013) provides a detailed discussion of the potential and pitfalls of crowdsourcing translation in a crisis. Marlowe (2020) highlights that transnational networks are part of refugees' everyday lives and that social media platforms can provide access to trusted translated communications to these communities during times of crisis. He distinguishes between 'crisis-near' and 'crisis-far' events and illustrates how social media can be used by refugees to warn and provide support to their transnational networks.

In 2021 it has become crystal clear to the entire world how important information is in responding to a global pandemic. COVID-19 was, to use Marlowe's words (2020), both a 'crisis-near' and a 'crisis-far' event in that the entire world was affected and infected, as travel across boundaries aided the virus's transmission, which in turn led to international, national and local control measures. This happened in the physical world that we occupy. COVID-19 was, at the same time, a pandemic that occurred in the parallel space of the online world. In fact, national and local restrictions forced many people and activities online that previously only, or mainly, took place in physical spaces. We shared our information, experiences and emotions online and, of course, we did this in multiple languages and sometimes via translation. COVID-19 created a parallel pandemic space that was mediated via translation, sometimes with positive and sometimes with negative outcomes.

Communication, influence and trust in social media networks

Though the networked communicative spaces of social media can be thought of as parallel to the material spaces we exist in, they are closely interlinked. We routinely rely on social media to keep connected with family members, friends and co-workers, and this has only intensified with the minimization of face-to-face contact during the pandemic restrictions. Therefore, understanding how communication happens and how information travels on social media demands that we attend to the dynamics of these networked spaces, where interactions and communities are restructured by the affordances of digital technologies.

boyd (2010) proposes a useful conceptual model for understanding social media sites as networked publics restructured by digital technologies. These publics become simultaneously the space constructed by those technologies and the imagined community that forms 'as a result of the intersection of people, technology, and practice' (39). These constellations of users, technologies and practices give rise to certain dynamics, such as the blurring of public and private contexts and the possibility of accidental or intentional communicative context collapse (Davis and Jurgenson 2014) between different social groups, including in multilingual communicative spaces.

We propose to apply the analytic lens of networked communication to examine social media spaces as networked publics where users communicate with each other and where specific users (nodes in the network) who act as translators play more important roles in how far information travels and how it is perceived by their networked communities. Adapting the classic two-step flow model of communication (Nisbet and Kotcher 2009; Choi 2015) to the networked environment, we critically explore the role of social media users in translating information during the pandemic, drawing on interview data collected from specific stakeholders during the COVID-19 pandemic.

The two-step flow model of communication (Nisbet and Kotcher 2009; Choi 2015) suggests that information in networked spaces does not always travel in linear, hierarchical ways, and highlights the important role of micro-influencers (Abidin and Brown 2018)—users who are well-connected across networks and enjoy a certain level of credibility or trust, as well as intimacy, within their immediate networked communities. Such micro-influencers or micro-celebrities (Tufekci 2013) do not always have large followings, but are perceived as authoritative figures by their peers and are often seen as key channels providing curated information about important political, social or cultural matters; as potential agents of mobilization (Tufekci 2013); and as role models guiding decision-making, including in crisis situations (Buijzen et al. 2021). They can serve as 'bridges' between parallel networked spaces and can use social media as a connector between official communication channels (government, health authorities, etc.) and community members that are often disconnected from these formal channels. It is therefore of utmost importance that official crisis communication efforts include the identification of such influencers and the establishment of rapport with them as key message carriers of official information to their communities, whose members often exist in parallel communicative spaces due to contextual, knowledge or language barriers.

The use of micro-influencers to filter information to their networks and translate the key messages also represents a potential risk around misinformation and mistranslation. Another potential risk in terms of official government communication in crisis situations is the mis-identification of micro-influencers who could be 'bridges' between official institutions and specific communities, which can undermine trust instead of increasing it. The central role of trust-building in the context of translation efforts during crises thus becomes even more important.

Trust is a fundamental component of crisis communication for all stakeholders in all directions (Curnin et al. 2015; Wray et al. 2006; Paton 2007, 2008; Steelman et al. 2015). Building trust prior to the onset of a crisis through sustained contact between key stakeholders has been associated with effective communication during a crisis (Auf Der Heide 1989; Stephenson 2005). Trust can be invested in the source of the crisis communication as well as the content of the communication (Paton 2007, 2008) and increasingly intimate relations between the source and the receiver have been linked to higher levels of trust (Arlikatti et al. 2007).

Despite its importance, trust is complex and easily confounded with other concepts such as trustworthiness, cooperation or collaboration (Guinnane 2005; Zand 2016). There is wide agreement that trusting is a mechanism for dealing with uncertainty, risk or vulnerability (e.g. Hardin 2006; Luhmann 1988; Nooteboom 2002; Möllering 2006). One influential review of trust literature proposes a typology of different forms of trust (Rousseau et al. 1998) and depending on the scholar's academic orientation—e.g. cognitive, economic, political, social, etc.—they may focus on a different form. Those with a social orientation may tend to examine trust in terms of its relational and institutional aspects (Rousseau et al. 1998). In all forms and at all levels, social trust is dynamic and contextual (Zand 2016). Social trust should be analysed within the boundaries of a particular setting or context—in our case, also the context of communities exchanging information in social media spaces.

In summary, we have argued that trust is central to crisis communication. Theories of social trust can be used to describe and explain how migrants decide to make themselves vulnerable or not to sources of pandemic communication by considering the parameters of the communicative context. We now further examine the circulation of crisis information among networked publics, the role of micro-influencers in translating COVID-19-related information and the factors affecting trust in these translation dynamics.

Analysis and discussion

We carried out a study between June and November 2020 to understand the use of translation in Ireland's COVID-19 crisis communication and its role in behaviour change among diverse language communities in Ireland (for a full report on this see O'Brien et al. 2021). As part of this study, we conducted interviews with nine stakeholders representing: (1) Commissioners of translated content; (2) providers of translated content; and (3) recipients of translated content, all of whom were living in Ireland during the pandemic. More specifically, we secured interviews with:

- A representative of Ireland's Health Service Executive (HSE), which along with the Department of Health leads the government's public communication campaign around COVID-19;
- A representative of one of the language service providers contracted by the HSE to translate content during the pandemic;
- Two Brazilian nationals living in Ireland who had limited English proficiency (LEP);
- Four representatives of not-for-profit organizations operating in Ireland that deal directly with migrant workers and asylum seekers;
- One academic who specializes in minority languages, in this case Irish.[1]

We conducted semi-structured interviews online via Zoom with participants (lockdown restrictions prevented in-person meetings at the time). Each interview lasted between approximately 30 and 60 minutes and dealt in general with the crisis-related information needs of users of languages other than English in Ireland and evaluation of how these needs were satisfied or not during the crisis. Interviews were recorded, transcribed, confirmed by participants, and then coded using a phased, multicoder approach based on discussion, agreement and recoding. Ethical approval for this project was received from the institutional research ethics committee and all participants provided their informed consent prior to the interviews.

Our interviews did not seek to focus on the role played by social media and translation during the pandemic, but social media inevitably emerged as a topic. Three themes in particular emerged from our data, which we use here to frame our discussion on parallel pandemic spaces:

- Use of social networks and why they are important during a crisis.
- The importance of trust in the source, not just in the content.
- The importance of trust-building as a form of preparedness.

Use of social networks and why they are important during a crisis

We noted previously how social networks can be used in general to keep in touch with family, friends, co-workers, etc. during 'normal' times. Face-to-face contact was severely impeded during the worst waves of the COVID-19 pandemic and citizens increasingly turned to digital tools to maintain contact with their networks, creating an even more important parallel space during the pandemic. The need went beyond the normal human requirement for social contact to a need for information, understanding and reassurance. If one is a migrant in a foreign country, physical social circles might already be quite limited and so the isolation of a pandemic lockdown is even more severe. One would understandably turn to a parallel online space to seek information and reassurance. As one of our interviewees (P2) noted:

> [...] a lot of [...] people forget that you can live in a country like Ireland as a migrant and not chat to an Irish person for a week. Maybe somebody behind the shop counter or on the bus but other than that, all your mates can be from the same place, your television at home can be, you know, online. You can be watching TV from wherever [...]

A migrant worker who took part in our interviews (P5) confirmed that she was using social media (Instagram, Facebook) for information seeking purposes and that she would have liked to have had some subtitles for some of the content in English:

> I believe social media is the easiest way to have access to all the information, and it's the way that I use personally. I have easier access to it and if they could provide some sort of subtitles as well, in those social media, that would be very helpful.

Due to the language barrier, she was sourcing most of her information during the pandemic on social media from 'Brazilian sources', indicating that online communicative spaces can often stretch beyond the immediate local or national context.

NGO organizations who typically provide services to such communities also confirmed that they communicated via social media platforms during the pandemic:

> So we thought the only way we could actually re-engage with our clients in this pandemic is, as I said this week, we've introduced, you know, contacting them twice a week. We've used WhatsApp, we've used emails, we've used phone calls. So it reassures them that they're not left alone. It reassures them in terms of new information published by the government. And it reassures them that our services are still there as well as the government's (P4).

However, the same interviewee (P4) mentioned that WhatsApp was also being used for the dissemination of misinformation, which had been curated from sources in the migrants' home countries. The pandemic had different effects around the world at different times and so information from one country did not necessarily pertain to another. Yet, that information was being harvested and disseminated among online networks, with potentially negative outcomes. In relation to Brazilian migrant workers in Ireland, for example, P2 stated:

> Their main contact is with home and at home, they are being told there's nothing to worry about, this thing could be a hoax. And so that, you know, that impacts their behaviour locally then and that can be so divisive potentially in our community because people don't understand […]

This provides a snapshot of some of the confirmation our interviewees provided for the use and importance of social media during the COVID-19 pandemic in Ireland, where it was used to maintain connections in an online world, but was also a source of locally irrelevant or even contradictory information.

Importance of trust in the source, not just in the content

The global nature of the pandemic, coupled with ease of access to international information through digital platforms, including social media, meant that people could access information in many languages, some of which they needed to translate. The issue of trust arose on numerous occasions in our interviews. One interviewee (P5) stated that she generally trusted the information she read on Facebook, except for some 'sensationalist' individuals whom she then ceased to follow.

Noting that migrants are not necessarily plugged into the national, traditional media channels, another participant recorded how it was necessary to create content for dissemination to migrant communities in Ireland who were either not receiving the correct information (due to sourcing it online from abroad) or because they faced language barriers. The COVID-19 World Service was set up to address this issue: medical practitioners working in Ireland but originating from a variety of countries were asked to record translated video messages in their languages for dissemination to those language communities via WhatsApp. This approach not only broke through the language barrier, but also through an invisible trust barrier by presenting information via social media in translation through 'community bridges', or micro-influencers who have a similar identity to those being targeted. As P2 highlights:

> There's something, there's something powerful in [...] See- seeing like a doctor [...] so if I was [...] We got like the doctors to say, I'm Doctor X working in Cavan, or I'm Doctor whatever working in Cork, you know what I mean? You base them in Ireland. You base them in a local [...] So the person watching the video who is a long way from home and feels kind of, especially at the moment, is quite isolated. There's a feeling of 'oh thank God'. I mean, there's a respect or something or there's a [...] that person's [...] and we're together in this. I don't know [...] That is more than language. It's more than information. It's belonging, and with that sense of belonging I think the person buys into the national approach to this thing.

Inevitably, those who were struggling to understand the information being broadcast in their adopted countries turned to machine translating information that was posted on social media. One of the migrant workers interviewed mentioned using Google Translate, despite the fact that she did not really trust it: 'I use a lot Google, which I shouldn't [...] Because it's a really literal translation, so sometimes I put a phrase in there and I can see that it's totally not working, and that's why I really don't trust it' (P9).

It is not only technology that is mistrusted, however, but also the State as a source of information. In some countries, the majority of the population would trust information provided by official government sources. In others, where corruption is rife, for example, people might be less trusting of government-issued information. This level of mistrust can be imported when a person migrates to a new setting, forcing them to seek alternative sources of information, possibly via social media. One of our interviewees (P1) spoke about having to 'really work with community leaders to [...] get messages out'. Furthermore, migrants may have experienced very difficult journeys getting to countries where they seek asylum and these journeys, and their encounters along the way, including in their host countries, may also have eroded their ability to trust people in power, leading them to seek trusted sources back home through social media.

This data from our interviews underlines that trust in information plays an important role in a crisis in general, but, as mentioned previously, trust is a complex topic. Here we have shown that many factors contribute to the calculation of trust in translated communication via social media, including the source of the information (people or technology), how close a communicator is in identity to the targeted recipient, and prior experience of interactions with state or government authorities.

Trust building via social media as a form of preparedness

Preparedness is a key component in Disaster Risk Reduction (Paton 2003). We can expect that disasters will occur and that they will be of different scales across varied timelines. We also understand that one disastrous event (or a smaller-scale crisis) can have cascading effects, a recent example being the 2011 Great East Japan Earthquake (Norio et al. 2011; McGee et al. 2016). Some disasters are more predictable than others. Nonetheless, we can be prepared for those that we know are likely to occur. Despite predictions and warnings (Morens et al. 2020; MacKenzie 2020), the global COVID-19 pandemic found many countries in various states of unpreparedness. One of the learnings we can take from this pandemic is that we need to be prepared for translating crisis communication.

We understand the relevance and importance of social media as tools for crisis communication and as networked publics (boyd 2010). Taking the two-step flow model of communication (Nisbet and Kotcher 2009; Choi 2015), which highlights the important role of micro-influencers in establishing trust, we can propose the use of micro-influencers as translators for crisis preparedness via social media. Evidence of this line of thinking was already emerging from our interview data. For instance, P8 who works with a migrant rights group in Ireland outlined their model as:

> [...] to really ensure that gatekeepers and leaders in communities have the information and that information is then shared amongst

family and friends networks, kind of like targeted Facebook ads, translated as well [...]

P8 went on to emphasize that the 'gatekeepers' had to be 'trusted voices' in the community. It is logical to add that those trusted translating voices must have a presence in the parallel physical and digital spheres in their communities, especially in a crisis such as a pandemic.

P7, a representative of an information service provider to migrants and refugees in Ireland, highlighted the importance of the micro-influencers, too:

> We have amazing technology these days to produce, you know, a place where people can go for information. And it would be really useful for us, as service providers, to have something to rely on. And I think service providers would absolutely take that to heart and would want to promote that. So, you know, that would be a mechanism of *creating trust*, by having that *referral pathway* from some *organizations that were already trusted* (emphasis added).

It is difficult to establish these 'referral pathways' during the response stage of a crisis when chaos can reign, which brings us back to the topic of preparedness. Emergency response organizations need to first recognize the need for translation in crisis situations. They then need to (continuously) assess the language and communication needs by examining language and literacy barriers and, not least, they need to establish bridging relationships through trusted stakeholders for those communities, online and physically, as a form of preparedness.

Alternative pathways might seem viable, but COVID-19 demonstrated that, at least in Ireland and probably in many other countries, traditional pathways for disseminating information were not adequate for migrant communities. For example, many migrants in Ireland did not have a relationship with their GP (General Practitioner, or doctor–P7), they had never heard of the HSE, nor could they easily find the translated information in 26 languages on the HSE website, and they most likely did not watch or listen to the national broadcasting channels where much of the information was being disseminated (P2). A significant number of these migrants hold jobs that continued to operate during the pandemic (e.g. public transport, meat-processing plants). There was some reliance, then, on employers to disseminate information, but one of our migrant workers (P9) noted: 'I did trust the social media even more, to be honest, because it was quicker. The employer, it took so long in between the communications [...] So that's why I kind of trust the internet more'.

Community organizations have a very important role to play here, too. As an example of trust-building prior to the pandemic, P2 described the organization called 'Sanctuary Runners' which was established in 2018 in Ireland (sanctuaryrunners.ie; @SanctuaryRunner), to offer solidarity, friendship and respect—through running—to people who had arrived in Ireland seeking asylum (these people are housed in what are called 'Direct Provision Centres'[2]). There was a connection between this group of people and the COVID-19 World Service, mentioned earlier. P2 highlights the essential trusting link between the running group and the dissemination of translated videos during the pandemic, which was facilitated via social media:

> [...] the Sanctuary Runners is about 2000 sanctuary runners, right, so this is very specifically to do with direct provision centres. So we'd have about five or six hundred people in direct provision centres who run with us or hang out with us or who know us and who trust us and we [...] they know we're not doing it out of charity. It's very much a solidarity thing. So there is trust in there, you know, so this, that was particularly useful when we were doing the videos before this service, you know what I mean? People would trust us where they wouldn't necessarily trust somebody from the government department [...].

While not planned as a formal type of preparedness, it is clear that this community initiative contributed to the building of trust relationships prior to the pandemic, which were then leveraged for good during the pandemic itself. Initiatives like Sanctuary Runners tend to exist in parallel spaces, too. While they congregate in a physical location to run, they also use social media to coordinate their physical activities, stay in touch, share and deepen their connections. They constitute readymade networks of communication and trust that can be leveraged as spaces for crisis translation.

Translated crisis information might be posted by official service providers via social media, as well as through traditional channels such as print, radio, etc. The service providers need to engage professional translators, or sometimes interpreters, to produce these translations and consequently need to have trusting relationships with those professionals. Indeed, we found that having a Standard Operating Procedure (SOP) in place between the HSE and their Language Service Provider prior to the onset of the pandemic contributed significantly to a trusting relationship that facilitated speedy production of professional translation (O'Brien et al. 2021). The argument is often put forward in professional and academic translation settings that 'non-professionals'—or at least what they produce—cannot be trusted. Detailed discussion on this debate is beyond the scope of this chapter, but it is interesting to note that the opposite view was held by some interview participants:

> Some of the work we do has volunteer interpreters, as in, like, kind of friends and family, which, you know, played a lot of different roles in meetings with workers. There's a lot of trust involved there. There's, you know, information [...] you're able to get the working terms and conditions. Just because there's a lot of trust in the room (P8).

> I think it's so much better if you, if we had an interpreter that ended up being from the same town as someone's cousin. And then that kind of, I think there is a different level of trust (P8).

At the same time P8 recognized that much depended on the context of the communication and if, for example, legal information was being disseminated then 'you have to have that kind of professional consecutive interpreting'. This counter-view reminds us that trust is dynamic and contextual (Zand 2016). For crisis contexts, trust-building needs to take place as a form of preparedness, which involves the identification of trusted voices as micro-influencers within communities and their preparation for occupying and connecting parallel pandemic spaces, when required.

Conclusion

This chapter has sought to highlight the essential role played by social media networks in disseminating translated information throughout the COVID-19 pandemic. More than simply highlighting the importance of this medium, we aimed to raise awareness of the intricacies of translated communications in social media and the potential challenges they pose. We first noted how social media enable us to create parallel online spaces and communities in general, then turned attention to how the global characteristics of the pandemic, as well as the local physical lockdowns, enhanced the need for these parallel pandemic spaces. The need for accurate and timely *local* information was high, but language proved to be a barrier for some, pushing them towards information-seeking in other languages, from other jurisdictions, as well as towards the need for translation, much of which was facilitated via social media. However, ease of access to information in a language that can be understood from another geographical location potentially led to disinformation, or at least information that was not relevant for the physical space occupied by the information-seeker, which emphasizes the need for translation of locally relevant crisis information via social media, among other platforms.

We documented, through interview data from the Irish COVID-19 context, that social media platforms were indeed used by migrants and service providers for those communities. Trust emerged as a major consideration and is a complex and context-dependent commodity, influenced by the source of the information, the context and prior experience. Trust cannot be constructed in a crisis simply by using professional translators or interpreters, especially not for social media content. This challenges the notion held in professional and academic settings that professional translation is the only ethically acceptable model in a crisis context. Social media users will translate at will, using friends, neighbours and machine translation (MT) systems, or they may bypass the need for translation by sourcing information from their home countries, potentially resulting in misleading and dangerous advice. Trust needs to be established as a crisis preparedness action so that social media crisis communication can be effective. Examples of how this can be achieved include grassroots community integration initiatives and the identification and onboarding of translating micro-influencers by those responsible for crisis communication. Professional translation and interpreting play a role for some contexts, but cannot be an exclusive strategy for chaotic, rapidly changing, life-threatening situations. Additionally, we have noted elsewhere (Federici et al. 2019) the need for *two-way* communication in a crisis (symbiotic exchange as mentioned by Desjardins 2017), something that is very easily facilitated from a technical perspective on social media. The concept of 'bridges'—trusted influencers who liaise between communities and service providers—is ideal here.

We close by acknowledging that there is a risk associated with this approach as those who present themselves as 'bridges' or influencers may not necessarily be accepted by targeted communities, or by all members of those communities, or may not be adequate translators of information. As with all crisis communication initiatives, no one channel should be relied upon and proper preparedness also includes gaining contextual knowledge of target communities and their needs.

Acknowledgements

The data acquisition for the interviews was funded by the DCU Educational Trust as part of the Rapid Response Research Hub for COVID-19.

Notes

1 We refer to our interviewees here as 'P1', 'P2', etc. for participants 1, 2 and so on.
2 For more information about Direct Provision Centres in Ireland, see https://bit.ly/3cybRS1

References

Abidin, C., and Brown, M. L. (2018). 'Introduction', in C. Abidin and M. L. Brown (Eds.), *Microcelebrity Around the Globe*, Bingley: Emerald Publishing Limited, 1–18.

Arlikatti, S., Lindell, M. K., and Prater, C. S. (2007). 'Perceived stakeholder role relationships and adoption of seismic hazard adjustments', *International Journal of Mass Emergencies and Disasters* 25(3): 218–256.

Auf Der Heide, E. (1989). *Disaster Response: Principles of Preparation and Coordination*, St. Louis, MO: Mosby.

boyd, d. (2010). 'Social network sites as networked publics: Affordances, dynamics and implications', in Z. Papacharissi (Ed.), *A Networked Self: Identity, Community and Culture on Social Network Sites*, New York and Abingdon: Routledge, 39–58.

Buijzen, M., Anschütz, D., de Leeuw, R. N. H., Bleize, D. N. M., Sadza, A. J. C., de Droog, S. M., and Rozendaal, E. (2021). 'Behind the policy frontline in the Netherlands during the Corona crisis', *Journal of Children and Media* 15(1): 49–54.

Cadwell, P. (2020). 'Trust, distrust and translation in a disaster', *Disaster Prevention and Management – Special Issue on Translation in Cascading Crises* 29(2): 157–174.

Choi, S. (2015). 'The two-step flow of communication in Twitter-based public forums', *Social Science Computer Review* 33(6): 696–711.

Curnin, S., Owen, C., Paton, D., Trist, C., and Parsons, D. (2015). 'Role clarity, swift trust and multi-agency coordination', *Journal of Contingencies and Crisis Management* 23(1): 29–35.

Davis, J. L., and Jurgenson, N. (2014). 'Context collapse: Theorizing content collusions and collisions', *Information, Communication & Society* 17(4): 476–485.

Desjardins, R. (2017). *Translation and Social Media: In Theory, in Training and in Professional Practice*, London: Palgrave Macmillan.

Federici, F. M. (Ed.). (2016). *Mediating Emergencies and Conflicts*, London: Palgrave Macmillan.

Federici, F. M., and O'Brien, S. (Eds.). (2020). *Translation in Cascading Crises*, Abingdon and New York: Routledge.

Federici, F. M., O'Brien, S., Cadwell, P., Marlowe, J., Gerber, B., and Davis, O. (2019). *International Network in Crisis Translation – Recommendations on policies*, Deliverable 2.1 (INTERACT), http://doras.dcu.ie/23880/

Guinnane, T. (2005). *Trust: A Concept Too Many*, New Haven, CT: Economic Growth Center, Yale University.

Hardin, R. (2006). *Trust*, Cambridge: Polity.

Leeson, L. (2020). 'Ophelia, Emma and the beast from the east: Effortful engaging and the provision of sign language interpreting in emergencies', *Disaster Prevention and Management – Special Issue on Translation in Cascading Crises* 29(2): 187–199.

Luhmann, N. (1988). 'Familiarity, confidence, trust: Problems and alternatives', in D. Gambetta (Ed.), *Trust: Making and Breaking Cooperative Relations*, New York: B. Blackwell, 94–107.

MacKenzie, D. (2020). 'The covid-19 pandemic was predicted – here's how to stop the next one', *New Scientist* 247(3300): 46–50.

Marlowe, J. (2020). 'Transnational crisis translation: Social media and forced migration', *Disaster Prevention and Management – Special Issue on Translation in Cascading Crises* 29(2): 200–213.

McGee, S., Frittman, J., Ahn, S. J., and Murray, S. (2016). 'Implications of cascading effects for the Hyogo Framework', *International Journal of Disaster Resilience in the Built Environment* 7(2): 144–157.

Morens, D. M., Breman, J. G., Calisher, C. H., Doherty, P. C., Hahn, B. H., Keusch, G. T., Kramer, L. D., LeDuc, J. W., Monath, T. P., and Taubenberger, J. K. (2020). 'The origin of COVID-19 and why it matters', *The American Journal of Tropical Medicine and Hygiene* 103(3): 955–959.

Möllering, G. (2006). *Trust: Reason, Routine, Reflexivity*, Amsterdam: Elsevier.

Nisbet, M. C., and Kotcher, J. E. (2009). 'A two-step flow of influence? Opinion-leader campaigns on climate change', *Science Communication* 30(3): 328–354.

Nooteboom, B. (2002). *Trust: Forms, Foundations, Functions, Failures, and Figures*, Cheltenham: E. Elgar Pub.

Norio, O., Ye, T., Kajitani Y., Shi, P., and Tatano, H. (2011). 'The 2011 Eastern Japan great earthquake disaster: overview and comments', *International Journal of Disaster Risk Science* 2(1): 34–42.

O'Brien, S., and Federici, F. M. (Eds). (2020). *Disaster Prevention and Management – Special Issue on Translation in Cascading Crises* 29(2).

O'Brien, S., Cadwell, P., and Zajdel, A. (2021). *Communicating COVID-19: Translation and Trust in Ireland's Response to the Pandemic*, https://www.dcu.ie/sites/default/files/inline-files/covid_report_compressed.pdf

O'Mathúna, D. P., and Hunt, M. R. (2020). 'Ethics and crisis translation: Insights from the work of Paul Ricoeur', *Disaster Prevention and Management – Special Issue on Translation in Cascading Crises* 29(2): 175–186.

Paton, D. (2003). 'Disaster preparedness: A social-cognitive perspective', *Disaster Prevention and Management* 12(3): 210–216.

Paton, D. (2007). 'Preparing for natural hazards: The role of community trust', *Disaster Prevention and Management* 16(3): 370–379.

Paton, D. (2008). 'Risk communication and natural hazard mitigation: How trust influences its effectiveness', *International Journal of Global Environmental Issues* 8(2): 2–16.

Rousseau, D. M., Sitkin, S. B., Burt, R. S., and Camerer, C. (1998). 'Not so different after all: A cross-discipline view of trust', *Academy of Management Review* 23(3): 393–404.

Standage, T. (2013). *Writing on the Wall: Social Media – The First Two Thousand Years*, New York: Bloomsbury.

Steelman, T. A., McCaffrey, S. M., Velez, A. K., and Briefel, J. A. (2015). 'What information do people use, trust, and find useful during a disaster? Evidence from five large wildfires', *Natural Hazards* 76(1): 615–634.

Stephenson, M. (2005). 'Making humanitarian relief networks more effective: Operational coordination, trust and sense making', *Disasters* 29(4): 337–350.

Sutherlin, G. (2013). 'A voice in the crowd: Broader implications for crowd-sourcing translation during crisis', *Journal of Information Science* 39(3): 397–409.

Tesseur, W. (2020). 'Local capacity building after crisis: The role of languages and translation in the work of development NGOs in Kyrgyzstan', *Disaster Prevention and Management – Special Issue on Translation in Cascading Crises* 29(2): 214–226.

Tufekci, Z. (2013). '"Not this one": Social movements, the attention economy, and microcelebrity networked activism', *American Behavioral Scientist* 57(7): 848–870.

Wray, R., Rivers, J., Whitworth, A., Jupka, K., and Clements, B. (2006). 'Public perceptions about trust in emergency risk communication', *International Journal of Mass Emergencies and Disasters* 24(1): 45–76.

Zand, D. E. (2016). 'Reflections on trust and trust research: Then and now', *Journal of Trust Research* 6(1): 63–73.

5 Hello/Bonjour Won't Cut It in a Health Crisis

An analysis of language policy and translation strategy across Manitoban websites and social media during COVID-19

Renée Desjardins

Introduction

When COVID-19 had affected nearly all corners of the world, news stories began to report the pandemic's unequal effects on different demographics. In Canada, one of the largest initial outbreaks took place in Alberta in April 2020. The outbreak took hold in a meat-processing plant where a percentage of the workforce was 'staffed by people born and raised abroad', including temporary foreign workers and workers from the Filipino community in the province (Baum et al. 2020; Babych 2020). Language barriers were one of the challenges that led to 921 cases of COVID-19 at the Cargill High River plant: 'Bulletin-board postings and letters to employees were provided only in English, causing confusion about compensation, isolation protocols and eligibility for paid time off, workers said' (Baum et al. 2020). What this example speaks to is the fact that crisis[1] itself is not necessarily discriminatory: arguably, the COVID-19 pandemic has affected everyone, to varying degrees. However, the pandemic did underscore and continues to underscore 'inequitable *policies* and *institutions* that place those already at risk'—such as the meat-processing workers at the Cargill High River plant—'in perilous positions' (Clark-Ginsberg and Petrun Sayers 2020: 482). Indeed, when larger corporate or public communication strategies and language policy ignore the importance and value of translation, interpretation and multilingual communication, the burden is placed on already disadvantaged groups 'to bear the brunt of COVID-19 *information insufficiency* and *misinformation*' (Clark-Ginsberg and Petrun Sayers 2020: 482). For example, the Cargill High River employees combatted information insufficiency by

DOI: 10.4324/9781003183907-6

creating social media groups, notably on Facebook, that provided information in English and Tagalog (Baum et al. 2020).

There is no federal law that requires businesses in Canada provide communication in Indigenous languages (e.g. Cree) or languages related to migration (e.g. Tagalog), though section 3(c) of the *Canadian Multiculturalism Act*[2] suggests the Canadian government must endeavour to facilitate civic participation in 'all aspects of Canadian society' regardless of origin. With a narrow focus on official languages, federal, provincial, and corporate entities may have indeed fulfilled their obligation to serve some Canadians during the pandemic, but they did not reach all Canadians and Indigenous Peoples[3] and this continues to be the case at the time of writing, particularly with regard to vaccine rollout in Canada.

Canada's *Official Languages Act*[4] ensures the use and respect of the official languages of Canada (English and French) in federal institutions (and specifically, of interest here: in communicating and providing services to the public). However, as McDonough Dolmaya (2020: 553) indicates, 'translation is directly mentioned only three times: when referring to the proceedings of Parliament, regulations by the Governor General, and information added to bilingual forms used in federal court'. Notably absent from the *Official Languages Act* (at the time of writing[5]) are Indigenous languages and languages of migration. In the context of this crisis, the lack of translation into languages other than the official languages (such as Tagalog and Vietnamese) has been ostensibly deadly, which illustrates the concept of 'cascading crises' rather evocatively (Pescaroli and Alexander 2015; Federici and O'Brien 2019). The focus of this chapter is not to scope a revision of or to propose specific amendments to the *Official Languages Act*. Rather, I point to the lack of language protection for (and outright omission of) Indigenous languages and languages of migration to show how federal institutions (as well as other governing bodies) shape bilingualism and multilingual communication in Canada and how such language policies have effects elsewhere in terms of linguistic and translational justice.[6] In Canada, language policy also varies provincially: strategies differ and can be sector-specific and English remains largely dominant nationally, despite Canada's linguistic diversity.

Thus, Canadian citizens and residents can usually expect federal-level communication in English and French. At provincial level, communication will usually align with the province's official language (English *or* French), to the exception of New Brunswick (English *and* French). However, crisis communication follows a different logic than everyday communication and general public sector communication: there is a different sense of urgency and access to information should be easy and equitable. Said differently: current official federal and provincial policies do not suffice to ensure reach and equitable access to information at a time of crisis.

Reporting on the Cargill High River case indicated translation and interpretation should have been key strategies in navigating the pandemic in Canada, though neither was touted as a frontline strategy in the initial stages of the crisis. Further, it was increasingly clear that it was not only a matter of ensuring interlinguistic translation and interpretation, but cultural translation as well (Desjardins 2021b). In various reports, employees recounted having to maintain social/physical distance, yet carpooling and multigenerational living arrangements were commonplace. Such practices are not inherently problematic outside of a health crisis and they serve to create community and support systems within migrant or newcomer populations. However, Cargill failed to initially account for these factors in its communication to employees, assuming it was feasible to find alternative modes of transportation or housing and neglecting how culturally conflicting such recommendations might be. Employees from migrant and newcomer communities, specifically the Filipino community, felt 'unfairly blamed' (Dryden 2020) for the outbreaks. Even if employees could have mitigated risks associated with carpooling and multifamily households, the fact remains that meat processing itself is a close-proximity job.

Following these events, I decided to examine whether similar cases of non-translation were being reported in Manitoba. According to 2016 Census data (Statistics Canada 2017), the province had 288,985 Manitobans (22% of the population) who did not have English as their mother tongue and 144,800 Manitobans (11% of the population) whose most spoken language at home was neither of the official languages.[7] Manitoba was an outlier province in the early months of the pandemic: unlike other Canadian provinces, its case counts were low and some experts opined the province had been spared from the first wave that swept elsewhere across the country. However, in fall 2020, case counts increased significantly and reports began to surface across the province suggesting that language, outbreaks and public health communication were indeed intertwined. In October 2020, a Francophone daycare reported a COVID-19 case and parents received information of this in English (Radio-Canada 2020). For the daycare's director, whose fifth language is English, this posed a problem (Radio-Canada 2020). The daycare received information in French a day later, but the sentiment was that this was a little too late. This example shows the delay some non-English speakers had to face and accept in order to receive information in their languages. Further, it is worth noting in this case that the language in question was French, a *national official* language. It is reasonable to hypothesize the delay was likely longer for other languages without official languages status and that other cases of non-translation went underreported.

Canada's federal and provincial governments increasingly leveraged online social media to publicize important public health information, including epidemiological statistics, vaccination information and testing site locations. Canada, of course, was not unique in doing so—social media have increasingly replaced other forms of traditional media (e.g. television, radio) in providing news to the masses internationally. That said, Canada's specific language laws and policies do intersect with federal and provincial communication strategies, yet consensus on how this applies to social media remains to be determined, particularly in crisis. What is known is that there is a federal obligation and some provincial obligations to communicate critical information in both official languages.

The coverage of the Cargill outbreak in Alberta and local Manitoba reporting both revealed translation oversights (and arguably a lack of translational justice). Thus, I decided to further investigate the Government of Manitoba's online COVID-19 translation strategy. More specifically, the case study below focuses not so much on a comparative analysis of content translation (i.e. comparing English and French versions of a tweet), but rather in how translation—in the context of the COVID-19 pandemic—is accessed from the perspective of the user's experience (UX).[8] I start by examining the Government of Manitoba's website, followed by its social media accounts to identify translation strategies and translated/ multilingual content. I compare this analysis with 'conversations' on Twitter, relative to the handling of the pandemic and vaccine rollout. The goal is to map some of the social conversations about the pandemic, translation, multilingual communication, and Manitoba in order to see how public health discourse and translation in crisis situations intersect (cf. Federici and O'Brien 2019; O'Brien 2011, 2016). This case study intends to expand research on multilingualism, language barriers, linguistic and translational justice in Canada beyond the 'Bilingual Belt' (a corridor that spans roughly from Montreal to Toronto). It is worth noting that translation studies research produced in and about Manitoba remains limited.

Government of Manitoba websites and socials: Case study

Theoretical framework and methodology

This chapter constitutes a context-oriented case study that examines both qualitative and quantitative data related to translation on social media, language demographics, and the COVID-19 pandemic in Manitoba.

I collected data using different approaches and tools, in line with current practices in the Digital Humanities.[9] This includes web scraping, hashtag indexing/searching, network analysis and close-reading/ discursive analysis of specific social media content and accounts, including searches for multilingual features and content, however these occurred (e.g. 'translate' buttons, hyperlinks to translated documents, bilingual account information). When conducting online research, particularly in the context of crisis, it is important to take into account some ethical considerations, such as objectifying traumatic experience or personal accounts without explicit consent, even if the content is public-facing. More specifically, three areas warrant attention: general ethics, privacy and security. While a detailed discussion of all three areas escapes the scope of this chapter, it is worth noting that this case study falls under observational work for which only public-facing data was examined; otherwise, sensitive information has been anonymized or omitted in compliance with guidance from the Canadian Tri-Council Policy statement.[10] Online communication can ephemeral and fast-paced, so it can also be difficult to track content in real-time and over time (Desjardins 2017): I acknowledge this posed a challenge. The findings I present here are current at the time of writing.

The study of translation in online contexts[11] also requires a re-assessment of 'traditional' categorizations of translational phenomena. Within the field, there is a tendency to approach different types of translation as wholly distinct from one another, for instance, some researchers view audiovisual translation as distinct from online social translation. However, the multimodal nature and layered 'materialities' (cf. Littau 2015) of digital online contexts 'necessarily multiplies the forms translation activity can take' (Desjardins 2021a: 131). If one is to examine translation in online contexts, one has to concede that the lines between human translation, neural MT, crowdsourced translation—to name only these—become increasingly blurred, especially depending on the viewpoint (Desjardins 2019). For instance, depending on a user's settings and preferences, social media content might only appear in one language, while other users may choose to use a localized version of the platform, while others, still, might select other language preferences, such as automated translations without prompts. As such, when I analyze translation in social media contexts, I opt for a holistic approach that takes into account all (or as many as methodologically feasible) types of translation concurrently taking place.

Unsurprisingly, the COVID-19 pandemic has created an impetus for projects that seek to make sense of the crisis and to propose ways to mitigate detrimental effects and injustices in the future. One particular area that has warranted significant attention—as some of the chapters in this volume signal—has been the nexus of social media, misinformation and disinformation. This is understandable, given that social media play a crucial, and sometimes misunderstood or understudied role in the proliferation of dubious and misleading content.[12] For instance, Gruzd and Mai (2020) studied the propagation of COVID-19 conspiracy theories on social media. Their goal was to understand how a hashtag (#FilmYourHospital) can 'travel' through a network. The authors conclude that the more notoriety a misleading claim gains, the harder it is to 'root out' misinformation/disinformation. However, an emphasis on misinformation/disinformation obfuscates other informative observations from social media data. In the case of the Cargill High River outbreak in Alberta, misinformation did not inherently lead to more cases; rather, it was the lack of a comprehensive multilingual, cross-cultural communication strategy at a time of crisis and a lack of knowledge around the novel coronavirus itself. The Filipino Facebook groups initially created by Cargill employees, for example, were helpful in tipping reporters to a lack of multilingual communication at the plant and within larger communities. This is why the theoretical lens of translational justice/linguistic justice (De Schutter 2017; McDonough Dolmaya 2020; Desjardins 2021a) is appropriate for this study. Language and translation policy inform practice, behaviour and output, and provide a sense of what citizens can expect. The analysis of policy, strategies and output (content created by institutions), and interaction (user engagement/ user experience) can shed light on best practices and omissions—that is, where translational justice is served and where it is not. Policies codify the status of languages and structure communication with and within the public. What the COVID-19 global pandemic has underscored is the need for concerted and consistent multilingual public health messaging to help guide citizens through different phases of crisis and different public health measures. When the logic of official languages is applied to public messaging at a time of crisis, to the erasure or outright omission of other languages, parts of the population who do not speak or who have less proficiency in the official languages stand to be considerably less informed than those who are proficient. This creates an asymmetry in actionable knowledge and can lead to or exacerbate other underlying inequities (social, economic). In the words of Rodríguez Vázquez and Torres-del-Rey (2019: 93): '[...] speaking a different language [...] or simply coming from a different cultural background could make the person "informationally vulnerable" or disabled, given that accessing needed information would represent a challenge in its own right unless translation and/or interpreting services were to be available'.

Analysis

I first examined the Government of Manitoba website followed by its official social media accounts, with particular attention given to COVID-19 content. Although Manitoba is not considered officially bilingual, section 23 of the *Manitoba Act*[13] stipulates English and French have official status in the legislative and judicial spheres of government in the province.[14] *The Francophone Community Enhancement and Support Act* was assented in 2016 and its purpose is to 'provide a framework for enhancing the vitality of Manitoba's Francophone community and supporting and assisting its development through the work of the secretariat and the advisory council and the use of French-language services plans'.[15] Manitoba's Francophone Affairs Secretariat's French-Language Services Policy[16] states that its purpose is 'to allow [...] access [to] comparable government services in the language of the laws of Manitoba'. And, in relation to the provision of health services more specifically, the French-Language Services Policy also states that the same directives apply to public health bodies.[17] The policy does not explicitly outline social media communication guidelines, though one could surmise social content would fall under official Government of Manitoba communications and thus should be in both official languages. Similarly, the Winnipeg Regional Health Authority's (WRHA) 2019 Community Assessment Health Report (2019: 69) states that access to health services in one's language is an important social determinant of health and that miscommunication can be life-threatening.

Given that Francophones do represent a linguistic minority in Manitoba, the Act and these policies reflect a degree of linguistic and translational justice. Yet, Census data show that in addition to the previously cited statistics (see Introduction), 16,285 Manitobans had no knowledge of either official language, and 15,840 Manitobans had neither official language as a mother tongue. In fact, 16,865 Manitobans (1%) responded having French as the most spoken language at home, compared to 144,800 Manitobans (11%) who indicated non-official languages as the most spoken at home (Statistics Canada 2017). This is not to suggest Francophones should not have access to services in French provincially. However, it does suggest that exaltation of official languages does not serve other linguistic demographics, which, in a crisis situation such as the pandemic, is ineffective and inequitable.

• Government of Manitoba website

Government websites are a way for people to access information about provincial services and activities. Websites also serve as a 'point of entry' to find related social media accounts. Iconographical elements or buttons will redirect users to the social accounts in question. This is why I chose to examine the Government of Manitoba website as a point of departure, even though some may argue websites are not universally categorized as 'social media'.[18] Upon entering the Government of Manitoba site,[19] users have the option to view the main page in English or in French, the only two language versions available. This is consistent with the language policies outlined above, but appears incongruous when compared to the linguistic and cultural demographic make-up of the province. Interestingly, the Government of Manitoba website does not use iconographic elements to redirect users to social platforms. Instead, on both the English and the French sites, users must scroll to the very bottom of the page where they will find different social platforms listed. These are: Twitter, Facebook, YouTube and Flickr. Before turning to social media, a few additional points related to the website are warranted. Given the Census data, a strategic and equitable translation strategy would at least help users who speak other languages (Indigenous languages or languages of migration in particular) find translated content more easily or quickly on the site. While it is true that the site tabs indicate only English and French, content in other languages does exist elsewhere on the site. In fact, three (not necessarily intuitive) mouse-clicks starting from the English homepage will redirect a user to a section called 'Resources and Links', where two sub-sections include explicit reference to COVID-19 materials (infographics, fact sheets, videos) in other languages. First, the *Social (Physical) Distancing Factsheet* can be found translated into eight languages: French, Traditional Chinese, Simplified Chinese, Korean, Low German, Punjabi, Arabic, and Tagalog. Second, further below, another sub-section titled 'Other Languages' redirects to a collection of silent (no audio) *Focus on the Fundamentals* YouTube videos on the Government of Manitoba's YouTube account. These videos are available in the following languages: Amharic/Ethiopian, Arabic, Cree, English, French, German, Hindi, Mandarin, Punjabi, Spanish, Tagalog, Ojibwe and Dene.

The availability of multilingual content suggests some consideration was given to various linguistic communities, but there are some issues worth noting. The first is that these videos focus only on one aspect of the pandemic, the 'fundamentals' (e.g. handwashing, social distancing), without more specific aspects of this relative to different cultural groups. Essentially, the videos appear to be nothing more than 12-second translated videos for which no cultural adaptation is present, meaning that there are no markers related to cultural specificity or any adaptation to account for specific cultural differences.[20] Videos such as these can be useful, but more nuanced content, adapted to address specific cultural community needs and concerns should be available. The second problem is that accessing this content is not intuitive or straightforward (and this from the perspective of a researcher who is fluent in both official languages and who has studied the website). For instance, on the English homepage, it would be more intuitive to have a menu or explicit button signalling where to click for a direct route to content in another language. Curiously, the French version of the site requires a different set of clicks to find this same multilingual content—as if whoever designed the site or uploaded content felt users who spoke other languages would likely default to the English website to click through rather than the French. This ignores the fact that some Manitobans may very well have language combinations, such as Arabic and French but no English proficiency. A citizen can use the same three clicks from the English homepage to 'land' on the COVID-19 'Resources and Links' page and then select 'Français' to access the French version of the page. However, in doing this, the multilingual content listed above disappears: the French page does not have the seven other translated *Social (Physical) Distancing Factsheets*, nor does it have the *Focus on the Fundamentals* video library. This is one example of the discrepancies between the English and the French versions of the site, but the larger issue has to do with the seemingly inconsistent distribution of multilingual content, particularly if we consider UX.

Ultimately, it is apparent from this example that accessibility and universal design principles are inconsistent across the site as communicational and interactional content cannot be intuitively accessed unless one is prepared to go through multiple clicks. The structure of the site also presumes proficiency in either official language, to the detriment of the various linguistic communities that only speak other languages.

• Government of Manitoba on social media: Facebook, Twitter and YouTube

Social media have increasingly become a way for users to engage with government content more easily than previous traditional channels and government institutions at all levels in North America are increasing uptake, albeit in different ways (cf. Zavattaro and Bryer 2016; Desjardins 2017). Returning to the social media accounts listed on the Government of Manitoba's homepage, one notes the Government of Manitoba is present on four social platforms, three of which will be analyzed here:[21] Facebook, Twitter and YouTube. Whether a user accesses the English or the French homepage of the website, all four social accounts are listed in the same fashion, at the bottom of the page. Unlike the two separate versions of the website, the Government of Manitoba's social media strategy employs a different approach. All three social media accounts post both English and French content, as opposed to separate accounts for English content and French content (i.e. 'sister' accounts). I argue this is a more accessible strategy in terms of aggregating content for English and French users at a time of crisis compared to some of the inconsistent approaches taken on the website, but it is not without issues either, as will be discussed shortly. As noted elsewhere, Indigenous languages and languages of migration do not feature prominently or regularly on Government of Manitoba socials. Some may suggest that these specific language and cultural communities may turn to social accounts created by and for their communities[22] rather than the main Government of Manitoba social accounts. This does warrant further investigation, but falls beyond the scope of this analysis. Regardless, if population reach and public trust are important to government, approaches that favour inclusion and representation are likely to be more effective.

The Government of Manitoba's Facebook page is followed by 58,709 users (as of 1 July 2021). The page's 'About' section is only available in English even if a user's Facebook language preferences are set to prompt automatic content translation. This was tested by altering language parameters and translation settings in the way that a user who speaks Spanish or Tagalog might have done so (again, with an eye to analyzing content from the perspective of UX). The Government of Manitoba's Facebook page regularly uploads posts, but they are not systematically bilingual, whether the content relates to COVID-19 or not. In terms of COVID-19 content, media bulletins, such as the *COVID-19 Bulletin* and the *COVID-19 Vaccine Bulletin* are systematically posted in separate, language-specific posts (English and French), with links redirecting users to the Government of Manitoba news release page in either English or French, depending on which language version of the link users click. Neither the *COVID-19 Bulletin* nor the *COVID-19 Vaccine Bulletin* is translated or available in other languages via the Government of Manitoba Facebook page or website.

The Government of Manitoba website Twitter link directs users to the @MBGov account, but it is worth noting other sector-specific Twitter accounts exist (e.g. @MBGovNews, @MBGovRoads, @MBGovParks). One might expect to find a public health account with a similar handle, but instead, Shared Health Manitoba is found under the handle @SharedHealthMB. Users trying to find the Shared Health Manitoba socials from the Government of Manitoba COVID-19 website are unlikely to find this information easily. It should be noted that the Chief Provincial Public Health Officer and the Medical Lead for the Government of Manitoba COVID-19 taskforce tweet under individual accounts separate from the MBGov accounts. This points to a disjointed social media strategy in the handling of COVID-19: users should be able to find information about provincial health and public health websites and accounts on the Government of Manitoba COVID-19 webpage[23] easily. Citizens shouldn't have to navigate across numerous social accounts to find clear, plain language messaging (i.e. Shared Health, the CPPHO, and the taskforce Lead, and the MBGov accounts). Before returning to the Government of Manitoba Twitter accounts, a brief analysis of the Shared Health Manitoba website shows that the site is available in English and French (a user can select either English or Français by clicking a button); no other language options appear to be available. Further, Shared Health tweets and re-tweets predominantly in English and its Twitter profile is exclusively in English. The same applies to the CPPHO and Medical Lead of the Vaccine Taskforce Twitter accounts. Returning to the Government of Manitoba's Twitter account, specifically the @MBGov account: tweets and re-tweets are predominantly in English, though French-language content does make a somewhat regular appearance (this seems to coincide with news releases as described above or re-tweets of French-language content from other accounts).

The Government of Manitoba's YouTube channel has 12,200 subscribers. The account has a designated *COVID-19* playlist (English), which features a total of 346 videos and indicates 506,701 total views (as of 2 July 2021).[24] The channel also has a *Bulletin sur la COVID-19* playlist (French), which features a total of 203 videos and indicates 1,372 total views (as of 2 July 2021). It is interesting to note the discrepancy between the English playlist total video count and that of the French playlist: bilingual and Francophone users might be prompted to ask 'what's missing' or 'why are there fewer videos in French', resulting in a feeling of mistrust or confusion. Engagement is also significantly lower for the French-language playlist. Although this may make sense given that Census 2016 data show there are fewer French speakers than English speakers in Manitoba, it may also point to the fact that this playlist was not adequately advertised among relevant French-speaking communities or demographics. From the perspective of UX, the *Bulletin sur la COVID-19* playlist does not feature on the YouTube 'Home' page of Government of Manitoba when the default settings are in English—which for many users is likely the case. The channel also features a *RestartMB* playlist, which is part of the larger *RestartMB* campaign launched in August of 2020.[25] Thus, while this playlist is not labelled explicitly with 'COVID-19' or 'pandemic', it nonetheless contains content that relates to the health crisis. No French equivalent of the *RestartMB* playlist is featured on the channel, though the campaign was and is bilingual (i.e. *RelanceMB* in French). The *RestartMB* playlist features a total of 32 videos and 1,691 views (as of 2 July 2021). The last update to this playlist was on 26 October 2020, which marked a pivotal moment in Manitoba's pandemic trajectory, the beginning of the second wave, and a time at which the *RestartMB* campaign came under critical scrutiny (Carrière 2020). The silent *Focus on the Fundamentals* multilingual videos on the Government of Manitoba website are not part of the *COVID-19* playlist and are marked as 'unlisted'. This means that if a user wanted to find the multilingual *Focus on the Fundamentals* videos discussed previously, they would not be able to by going to YouTube directly; users must click through the English Government of Manitoba website to access this content. Finally, there appears to be no other multilingual content on the channel pertaining to COVID-19, to the exception of sign language interpretation embedded in the news pressers included in the *COVID-19* playlist.

- Beyond the Government of Manitoba: Other Manitoban social accounts and COVID-19 conversations.

With a followship of approximately 39,900 followers, CBC reporter Bartley Kives was one of the prominent journalists (and Twitter accounts) Manitobans turned to for pandemic coverage. Kives tweets predominantly in English, but reported on language barriers and health inequities in his coverage and live tweeting of the Government of Manitoba pandemic press conferences. Scope limits a full analysis of Kives's pandemic tweeting. However, a tweet published on 2 June 2021 (see Figure 5.1) exemplifies the effects lack of translation, interpretation and access to multilingual public health information can have.

Bartley Kives ✔ @bkives · Jun 2   •••
Reimer: Part of the problem in conducting vax outreach in **Stanley** health
district is language.

She says there are significant numbers of **Spanish** & low-German speakers
in that area, which sits at 13 per cent vax uptake among people 18 and up.

Provincial 18-and-up average is 66%

♡ 9   ⟳ 2   ♡ 22   ⬆

Figure 5.1 Tweet from CBC reporter Bartley Kives (@bkives) on language
        barriers and vaccine uptake.

'Reimer' refers to Dr. Joss Reimer, the medical lead and official
spokesperson of the Government of Manitoba COVID-19 vaccine taskforce and Medical Officer for Manitoba Health and Seniors Care. As
Manitoba entered a catastrophic third wave in May 2021, public health
officials and other government officials urged Manitobans to get vaccinated (May 2021). As data began to indicate vaccine uptake trends, it
appeared some regions lagged behind others. Though anti-vaccination
sentiments and other forms of vaccine hesitancy are likely to be a factor, it
was also clear that part of the problem was a number of language barriers,
as evidenced by Dr. Reimer's statement during the June 2 press conference.[26] The Census data indicate Spanish was the language most
spoken at home for 5,695 Manitobans. The same data show German was
the most spoken language at home for 24,795 Manitobans (with an additional 465 for Germanic not included elsewhere). Combined, these figures represent roughly 2% of the province's population. Though 2% is a
low percentage value, it can represent an important ratio relative to vaccine uptake, particularly during a third wave that saw Manitoba patients
flown out of province for critical care. If language barriers were significant
enough to make headlines, one can then wonder why translation and
interpretation were not forefront issues in the early stages of pandemic
preparedness in the province.

As part of the vaccination campaign, Manitoba vaccination supersites
offered vaccinated individuals 'I'm COVID-19 Vaccinated' ('Je suis
vacciné[e] contre la COVID-19') stickers. These were available in English
and French, although their distribution seemed somewhat arbitrary based
on anecdotal accounts on social media and elsewhere. Nonetheless, the
stickers became a symbol of pride and hope and, for some, notably those
from the Franco-Manitoban community, the stickers were also an

opportunity to show linguistic allegiance, belonging and identity. When people feel represented and included, they are likely to participate in activities and behaviours that promote the collective good, and research on the topic abounds across disciplines. Andrew Unger, a Manitoban teacher, proposed that the Government of Manitoba COVID-19 vaccine taskforce add Low German (Plattdeutsch) to the vaccine sticker languages (Longhurst 2021) and the Government of Manitoba obliged, citing the move was likely to increase vaccine confidence and enthusiasm among a low-uptake demographic. Indeed, this seems to be the case, as Twitter users have shared photos of the translated sticker enthusiastically with noticeable engagement. Figure 5.2 shows an anonymized example of a tweet that garnered 283 likes, 28 quote tweets and 27 re-tweets.

Exciting day! Vaccine stickers in Low German... my grandparents first language. #ProtectMB #vaccine #manitoba #lowgerman

9:50 AM · Jun 23, 2021 · Twitter for iPhone

27 Retweets   **28** Quote Tweets   **283** Likes

Figure 5.2 Anonymized Tweet with picture of Manitoba's vaccine sticker in Low German.

Among the comments indexed in the quote tweets were phrases such as 'this is dope', 'this is cool', 'I applaud this' and 'I want one! My first language'. Though it is too early to tell whether the Plattdeutsch stickers will have a marked effect on vaccine uptake in southern Manitoba, social media engagement suggests growing enthusiasm for multilingual vaccination stickers and, by extension, vaccine uptake.

Conclusion

This chapter examines language policy and linguistic demographics in Manitoba relative to some of the translation strategies employed by the Government of Manitoba during the COVID-19 pandemic across its website and social media accounts (Facebook, Twitter and YouTube). This initial analysis is a step in better understanding how and when the provincial government used translation and multilingual communication to reach Manitobans during a significant health crisis that is still ongoing. It is evident that COVID-19 content in the two Canadian official languages (English and French) was more frequently posted, despite Census data showing the province's diverse linguistic make-up. Canadian (federal and provincial) language policy exalts the official languages, but fails in some respects to reflect the linguistic needs of a diverse population at a time of crisis, particular in online contexts where citizens are likely to seek public health information rapidly. From the perspective of a user's experience, the Government of Manitoba's haphazard translation strategy on its website and social platforms makes it all the more difficult to know what to expect and where to find multilingual and translated content. Future research could include interviewing participants to corroborate initial findings presented in this chapter.

The assumption that citizens can pivot to English or French because they have knowledge of an official language does not mean that this proficiency suffices when making health decisions. The Government of Manitoba could have been a national leader in adopting a consistent and coherent translation/multilingual strategy while simultaneously leveraging social platforms more effectively. Social media data (Statista 2021) show that Facebook continues to be the most dominant platform worldwide, so it makes sense for the Government of Manitoba to have a presence there. However, the Government of Manitoba is oddly absent on Instagram: it does have an account, with 2,233 followers, but no posts, and the Government website does not feature the Instagram link. This seems like a missed opportunity, given that Instagram allows for a number of interesting translation strategies (such as automated translation for captions) and the fact that Statista ranks it fifth among the most popular platforms.

Translation cannot be an afterthought in a pandemic; the effects of non-translation contributed to a serious outbreak in Alberta in the initial phase of the pandemic in Canada. In Manitoba, language barriers resulted in delayed public health information, asymmetrical knowledge dissemination, as well as slower vaccine uptake. Moreover, adopting a disjointed online translation strategy does nothing to facilitate access to critical health information. Finally, this case study shows that even when a country and a province have seemingly robust official languages policy, this does not guarantee *equitable* and *effective* multilingual communication in a crisis. Sometimes, Hello/Bonjour simply doesn't cut it.

Notes

1 Federici and O'Brien (2019) nuance the difference between 'disaster' and 'crisis'. Here, I follow their use and definition of 'crisis' and 'crisis situation' to describe the COVID-19 pandemic.
2 https://laws-lois.justice.gc.ca/eng/acts/c-18.7/page-1.html
3 I deliberately distinguish between 'Canadians' and 'Indigenous Peoples' to address the fact that some Indigenous groups in Canada do not wish to be described or qualified as 'Canadian' or belonging to Canada (i.e., 'our' or 'Canada's Indigenous Peoples').
4 https://laws-lois.justice.gc.ca/eng/acts/o-3.01/fulltext.html
5 Bill C-32 was introduced on 15 June 2021 and pertains to the modernization of the *Act*.https://www.canada.ca/en/canadian-heritage/campaigns/canadians-official-languages-act/introduction-bill.html
6 I borrow the term 'translational justice' from De Schutter (2017).
7 In the Winnipeg Health Region Community Health Assessment Report (Winnipeg Regional Health Authority 2019: 68), attention is given to Census data that reflects *knowledge of official languages* rather than data from the *language most spoken at home*. The report explains why knowledge of official languages was chosen instead of mother tongue (which the report describes as 'maternal language'), but this seems to conflate knowledge of an official language with actual proficiency or preference. I argue that *language most spoken at home* is a more helpful and significant data point, because it suggests language preference *and* proficiency. Health communication can be delicate and fraught when a patient or caregiver is unable to fully express themselves or fully understand what is being communicated to them. Again, this is why the Cargill High River case in the introduction is so evocative: many migrant workers *have knowledge of an official language,* but that does not necessarily mean that this knowledge suffices in crisis, nor does it excuse businesses and institutions making English or the official languages the default.
8 'User experience' can refer to a person's subjective experience of a system, product, or service. It can also refer to the principles that will guide the design and creation of a system, product, or service. For more see https://www.nngroup.com/articles/definition-user-experience/.
9 For a more detailed definition of the Digital Humanities, see Berry and Fagerjord (2017) as well as Gold (2011) and Gold and Klein (2016).

10 Canadian Institutes of Health Research, Natural Sciences and Engineering Research Council of Canada, and Social Sciences and Humanities Research Council, Tri-Council Policy Statement: Ethical Conduct for Research Involving Humans (2018) available at https://ethics.gc.ca/eng/documents/tcps2-2018-en-interactive-final.pdf

11 For a more detailed explanation of the differences between 'online' and 'digital' and why I use a combined term here, see Desjardins (2020).

12 Some researchers use the terms interchangeably, while others make a distinction. Here, I view these terms as distinct, with misinformation meaning inaccurate content that circulates regardless of an organic or explicit motive to deceive, while disinformation is a type of misleading information with intent to deceive or mislead. For more on contemporary issues related to social media and disinformation, see Starbird (2019).

13 The long title was repealed and 'Manitoba Act, 1870' substituted by the *Constitution Act, 1982.*

14 https://www.solon.org/Constitutions/Canada/English/ma_1870.html

15 https://web2.gov.mb.ca/laws/statutes/ccsm/f157e.php?query=search

16 https://www.gov.mb.ca/fls-slf/pdf/fls_policy_en20170908.pdf

17 http://www.gov.mb.ca/fls-slf/pdf/fls_policy_en20170908.pdf

18 The definition of social media varies among experts and across disciplines (Desjardins 2017).

19 https://manitoba.ca/index.html

20 For more on the concept of 'adaptation' and 'cultural translation', see Milton (2010), Marinetti (2011) and Conway (2012).

21 I intentionally omitted an analysis of the Flickr content because (1) the content does not pertain to the pandemic; (2) the last update to the content was in 2017; and (3) there is no evidence of interlinguistic translation that would be relevant here.

22 An example of a grassroots/community-based initiative would be the Protect Our People MB campaign, which has Facebook, Twitter and Instagram accounts. The campaign launched in May 2021 and is led by the Southern Chiefs' Organization Inc. (SCO), Manitoba Keewatinowi Okimakanak Inc. (MKO), Assembly of Manitoba Chiefs (AMC), Keewatinohk Inniniw Minoayawin, Inc. (KIM), the First Nations Health and Social Secretariat of Manitoba (FNHSSM) and the Manitoba government. At the time of writing, the Instagram account (@protectourpplmb) had 653 followers; its Twitter account 93 followers; and its Facebook page 174 likes.

23 Similar observations also apply for the Winnipeg Regional Health Authority's website (https://wrha.mb.ca/) and Twitter account (@WinnipegRHA). The Winnipeg Regional Health Authority represents a total population of approximately 750,000 Manitobans.

24 Some of the YouTube videos on the COVID-19 playlist do include sign language interpretation, but scope limits analysis of this here.

25 https://news.gov.mb.ca/news/index.html?item=49057

26 The video footage from the press conference is available in the COVID-19 playlist on the Manitoba government YouTube channel; Dr. Reimer's comments on language barriers occur at the 48:56 mark: https://www.youtube.com/watch?v=tN6y_36MfN8&list=PLvqXTqcYDg_fvIlP68aGxONh6DXfzsd0j&index=26

References

Babych, S. (2020). 'Filipino workers face backlash in towns over COVID-19 outbreaks at packing plants', *The Calgary Herald* (29 April, 2020), https://calgaryherald.com/news/filipino-employees-not-to-blame-for-meat-packing-plant-outbreaks-that-have-surpassed-1000-cases.

Baum, K. B., Tait, C., and Grant, T. (2020). 'How Cargill became the site of Canada's largest single outbreak of COVID-19', *The Globe and Mail* (3 May, 2020), https://www.theglobeandmail.com/business/article-how-cargill-became-the-site-of-canadas-largest-single-outbreak-of/

Berry, D. M., and Fagerjord, A. (2017). *Digital Humanities*, Cambridge: Polity.

Carrière, R. (2020). 'Not ready, not safe, not growing', *Winnipeg Free Press* (27 October, 2020), https://uml.idm.oclc.org/login?url=https://www-proquest-com.uml.idm.oclc.org/newspapers/not-ready-safe-growing/docview/2454302501/se-2?accountid=14569.

Clark-Ginsberg, A., and Petrun Sayers, E. L. (2020). 'Communication missteps during COVID-19 hurt those already most at risk', *Journal of Contingencies and Crisis Management* 28(4): 482–484.

Conway, K. (2012). 'Cultural translation', in Y. Gambier and L. van Doorslaer (Eds.), *The Handbook of Translation Studies*, Amsterdam: John Benjamins, 21–25.

De Schutter, H. (2017). 'Translational Justice: Between equality and privation', in G. González Núñez and R. Meylaerts (Eds.), *Translation as Public Policy: Interdisciplinary Perspectives and Case Studies*, New York and Abingdon: Routledge, 15–31.

Desjardins, R. (2017). *Translation and Social Media: In Theory, in Training and in Professional Practice*, London: Palgrave Macmillan.

Desjardins, R. (2019). 'A preliminary theoretical investigation into [online] social self-translation: The real, the illusory, and the hyperreal', *Translation Studies* 12(2): 156–176.

Desjardins, R. (2020). 'Online and digital contexts', in M. Baker and G. Saldanha (Eds.), *The Routledge Encyclopedia of Translation Studies*, Abingdon and New York: Routledge, 386–390.

Desjardins, R. (2021a). 'Are citizen science "socials" multilingual: Lessons in (non)translation from Zooniverse', in R. Desjardins, C. Larsonneur, and P. Lacour (Eds.), *When Translation Goes Digital*, London: Palgrave Macmillan, 121–152.

Desjardins, R. (2021b). 'Nutrition and translation', in S. Susam-Saraeva and E. Spišiakov (Eds.), *The Routledge Handbook of Translation and Health*, Abingdon and New York: Routledge, 385–402.

Dryden, J. (2020). 'Filipino workers at meatpacking plant feel unfairly blamed for Canada's biggest COVID-19 outbreak', *CBC* (26 April), https://www.cbc.ca/news/canada/calgary/cargill-high-river-jbs-brooks-deena-hinshaw-1.5545113

Federici, F. M., and O'Brien, S. (Eds.). (2019). *Translation in Cascading Crises*, Abingdon and New York: Routledge.

Gold, M. K. (Ed.). (2011). *Debates in the Digital Humanities*, Minneapolis, MN: University of Minnesota Press, 10.5749/9781452963754

Gold, M. K., and Klein, L. F. (Eds.). (2016). *Debates in the Digitals Humanities 2016*, Minneapolis, MN: University of Minnesota Press, 10.574 9/9781452963761

Gruzd, A., and Mai, P. (2020). 'Going viral: How a single tweet spawned a COVID-19 conspiracy theory on Twitter', *Big Data & Society* (July 2020), 10.1177/2053951720938405.

Littau, K. (2015). 'Translation and the materialities of communication', *Translation Studies* 9(1): 82–96.

Longhurst, J. (2021). 'Low German stickers sign of vaccine times', *Winnipeg Free Press* (28 June), https://www.winnipegfreepress.com/arts-and-life/life/faith/low-german-stickers-sign-of-vaccine-times-574723252.html

Marinetti, C. (2011). 'Cultural approaches', in Y. Gambier and L. van Doorslaer (Eds.), *The Handbook of Translation Studies*, Amsterdam: John Benjamins, 26–30.

May, K. (2021). 'Concerning trajectory: 251 new cases', *Winnipeg Free Press* (4 May), https://uml.idm.oclc.org/login?url=https://www-proquest-com. uml.idm.oclc.org/newspapers/concerning-trajectory-251-new-cases/docview/ 2521329835/se-2?accountid=14569.

McDonough Dolmaya, J. (2020). 'Translation and Canadian municipal websites: A Toronto Example', *Meta* 65(3): 550–572.

Milton, J. (2010). 'Adaptation', in Y. Gambier and L. van Doorslaer (Eds.), *The Handbook of Translation Studies*, Amsterdam: John Benjamins, 3–5.

O'Brien, S. (2011). 'Collaborative translation', in Y. Gambier and L. van Doorslaer (Eds.), *The Handbook of Translation Studies*, Amsterdam: John Benjamins, 17–20.

O'Brien, S. (2016). 'Training translators for crisis communication: Translators without borders as an example', in F. M. Federici (Ed.), *Mediating Emergencies and Conflicts: Frontline Translating and Interpreting*, London: Palgrave Macmillan, 85–111.

Pescaroli, G., and Alexander, D. E. (2015). 'A definition of cascading disasters and cascading effects: Going beyond the "toppling dominos" metaphor', *Planet@risk* 3(1): 58–67.

Radio-Canada (2020). 'COVID-19: Une garderie frustrée par la communication unilingue de la province', *Radio-Canada* (27 October), https://ici.radio-canada.ca/nouvelle/1744843/garderie-centre-soleil-covid-service-francais.

Rodríguez Vázquez, S., and Torres-del-Rey, J. (2019). 'Accessibility of multilingual information in cascading crises', in F. M. Federici and S. O'Brien (Eds.), *Translation in Cascading Crises*, Abingdon and New York: Routledge, 91–111.

Starbird, K. (2019). 'Disinformation's spread: Bots, trolls and all of us', *Nature* 571(7766): 449.

Statista (2021). 'Most popular social networks worldwide as of April 2021, ranked by number of active users', https://www.statista.com/statistics/272014/global-social-networks-ranked-by-number-of-users/

Statistics Canada (2017). *Manitoba [Province] and Canada [Country]* (table), *Census Profile* (2016 Census), Statistics Canada (Catalogue no. 98–316-X2016001), https://www12.statcan.gc.ca/census-recensement/2016/dp-pd/prof/index.cfm?Lang=E

Winnipeg Regional Health Authority (2019). 'Winnipeg Health Region Community Health Assessment', WRHA, https://wrha.mb.ca/files/cha-2019-full-report.pdf

Zavattaro, S., and Bryer, T. A. (Eds.). (2016). *Social Media for Government: Theory and Practice.* New York and Abingdon: Routledge.

6 On Memes as Semiotic Hand-Grenades

A conversation

Mª Carmen África Vidal Claramonte and Ilan Stavans

As a result of the COVID-19 pandemic, significant portions of human communication have moved online globally. Translation is no doubt a very important tool in social media, and for some decades up to now, translation scholars, some of them contributors in this volume, have analysed the connection between our discipline and the digital age. Among all these types of conversations, we have chosen memes. Memes are used in many fields of everyday life. They engage rational thinking and also touch our emotions. During the pandemic, they have spread faster than the virus and become viral. Some have been translated and travelled to different countries, but our starting point in this conversation is that an internet 'original' meme is not original but a translation.

Seen in this light, a dialogue between África Vidal (A.V.) and Ilan Stavans (I.S.), the internationally renowned semiotician, essayist, translator and the author of *Quixote: The Novel and the World* (2015), *I Love My Selfie* (2017) and *On Self-Translation: Meditations on Language* (2018), seems appropriate, since Stavans is a translator one could define as a translated translator, a polycentric, always-in-movement academic who uses different languages in his daily life, who is multi-layered, multicultural and a profoundly engaged intellectual with contemporary issues. In fact, he has just published an anthology on the pandemic, *And We Came Outside and Saw the Stars Again* (2020).

A.V: It is well-known that the term 'meme' was coined by Richard Dawkins in his 1976 book *The Selfish Gene*. As a concept related to sociobiology, memes show analogies with genes inasmuch as they are small units of cultural transmission that spread and replicate themselves as genes do. But Ilan, don't you think memes are today much more? In an article on memes (Stavans 2018b)

DOI: 10.4324/9781003183907-7

you refer to the origin of the word which draws on the ancient Greek *mimeme*, meaning 'something imitated', *mimeisthai* 'to imitate' and *mimos* 'mime'. In this vein, Sarah Maitland argued in a lecture entitled 'What can memes teach us about cultural translation?' (at the University of Edinburgh, 16 October 2019), that the construction of a meme 'becomes linked inextricably to ideas of playfulness, mimicry, emulation, imitation, verisimilitude, and metonymy. As cultural reproduction, memes make use of processes of copying and imitation' (Maitland 2019: n.p.). All these processes are essential in social media and digital spaces but are also the essence (or perhaps not) of translation.

I start this conversation on the premise of conceiving memes in translational terms. I think memes are not simply 'copying units' but translated cultural units which incorporate many layers and asymmetrical variations, and post topical comments out of the 'original' which modify its content and sometimes localize it. They sometimes even create new words. They are semiotic units that reconfigure, rewrite and translate contemporary issues based on an original (an image, a film, a song, a text) which the target audience recognizes. In fact, internet memes may function as cues of membership or serve as a sort of creative and social glue that bonds members of a community together (Cho and Suh 2021: 181). I think they exemplify Gentzler's (2015: 2) idea when he argues that the question of what constitutes a translation today is under radical review. The task of the translator no longer takes place between two languages but among 'many contemporary parts of social life. […] From this perspective, it is possible to view all language use as a process of translation, thus questioning the assumption that translation is a mapping of items from one code to another. […] [A]ll communication involves translation' (Otsuji and Pennycook 2021: 59). In this sense, memes could be interpreted as multimodal rewritings that refer to lively topics in the social media, or as Maitland (2019: n.p.) describes, as 'twenty-first-century palimpsests' that 'add new layers of meaning on top of the cultural phenomena they translate'. Would you agree?

I.S: Yes, memes are palimpsests, translated and translating artefacts created by layers of meaning. Memes are snippets of knowledge that carry, in their DNA, a vast cultural cosmos that viewers must decode first. This mechanism isn't unlike what takes place in parody: for the audience to appreciate the parodic message, it needs to appreciate what is being parodied. Think of *Don Quixote*. Most readers today have never read Amadís de Gaul, Tirant Lo Blac, or other chivalry novelist. Yet entering Cervantes's book, they immediately recognize how Don Quixote is an attempt at ridiculing them. Likewise with memes: upon receiving a meme that reconfigures a scene of *The Wizard of Oz*, viewers first recognize this 1939 classic film. Creators and recipients must share a common culture for the meme to be effective. But memes include another dimension: they are anonymous. In that sense, to me they are closer to folklore than to art: they are uncredited mechanical reproductions that, while created by an individual, are a product of the collective spirit seeking to give meaning, though the debris produced by internet communication, to the epistemological perplexity of a particular moment.

In my view, in 2020, especially during COVID-19 and as Donald Trump mastered tweets as the preferred method of dialogue with his political base, the meme, in my view, acquired truly global dimensions. As quarantine settled on the world's population, idle time pushed people to generate epistemic transactions across cultures that defied all types of borders, geographic, ideological and linguistic. The meme had been well-established long before; the pandemic simply emphasized its universal quality.

A.V: One of the first scholars in our field who used the concept of meme was Andrew Chesterman in his seminal book *Memes of Translation*, where he argues that memes are ways to translate ideas because they spread them but also change them. From a descriptivist perspective, Chesterman (2016: x) reminds us that translators are agents of change, since the meme metaphor gives 'less priority to the notions of "preserving identity" or "sameness" which underlie the more traditional image of "carrying something across", a something that somehow remains unchanged. I offer the meme metaphor as a helpful way to look at translation'. He views memes as concepts and ideas about translation itself, and about the theory of translation. He goes on to describe his five 'supermemes of translation', memes that encapsulate concepts and ideas on translation itself. This is, no doubt, an excellent starting point, especially because Chesterman underlies the fact that translation is not about sameness or mere equivalence. I would suggest going further in line with Lee and Chan (2018: 189), and starting from 'a dialogic view of translation premised on the notion of stimulus-and-response: translation responds to its source text (the stimulus), "talks back" to it, by developing and extrapolating the memes built into the latter, and it does so by way of mobilizing the signifying resources of the target language'. From this perspective, memes can be seen as units of translation of a rhizomatic nature. In line with Lee (2021: 12), memes could be seen as rewritings: 'different translations may choose to develop different memes from the same source text; or the same memes may be instantiated in divergent ways in different translations with recourse to their particular repertoires and the affordances available in the languages, modes, and media in use'. Can you think of other examples of literary memes?

I.S: Using literature again, memes are Menardian: just as Pierre Menard rewrites *Don Quixote* by recontextualizing it—the same exact words acquire an altogether different meaning once they are repeated—the meme extracts an epistemic unit of knowledge from its context and inserts it in another but does something more: it adds to its original meaning by inserting a caustic element that turns the original on its head. I remember years ago stumbling upon a volume in an Oxford bookstore of world literary classics (*Hamlet, The Adventures of Huckleberry Finn, The Great Gatsby*, etc.) delivered, in an abbreviated form, in tweets. Novelty aside, the question anyone interested in language and culture must ask is: can tweets generate the same emotional reaction in readers as full textual narratives might? Is the 'aesthetic moment' one experiences when following the existential odyssey of Prince Hamlet capable of being accessed in a sequence of 140-character messages, subsequently increased to 280? I ask this question because memes, while infused with satirical value, are still a language in its early stages of formation. Might a complex plot be composed one day through these linguistic bricks, which is another way of calling them?

A.V: You also say in your article I previously cited (Stavans 2018b) that the etymology of the word 'meme' is useful in that it points to artefacts as cultural capsules passing from one individual to another. I think this is a very important point because it makes us think about the idea that we live in 'The Age of Sharing', to use the title of Nicholas John's (2016) well-known book: sharing was once equivalent to caring, but in the digital age it is more related to what we do online, to a model of economic behaviour or to a type of therapeutic talk. In fact, during the pandemic, imagination helped to endure the lockdown. As you say in the introduction to *And We Came Outside and Saw the Stars Again* imagination helped us to 'escape mental imprisonment, some share memes, GIFs or tweets, while others recite poems, dress up, sing, talk on the phone or skype, dream, listen to the dreams of others. Thousands of artists have given away their plays, films, books and concerts online. The species persists through forms of representation of reality (eliminated from public budgets as the most expendable part of reality)' (Stavans 2020a: xvi–xvii). But sharing may not embody positive values and may be used to disguise racism, sexism and commercial or even exploitive relations.

I.S: It is indeed as you said. Social media is said to be a blessing and also a curse. In my case, it is more an affliction than anything else. Donald Trump: need I say anything else? When Facebook and Twitter took away his accounts, there was, expectedly, an outcry connected with First Amendment rights. But free speech, in the age of the internet, which creates silos of information, is no longer what it was in the eighteenth century, when the French Encyclopaedists reflected on the idea: it has turned individual rights into bastions of social disengagements. Social media in reality should be called *asocial* media: the age of sharing is also the age of minimizing others into misinformed soundbites. If we don't somehow curtail free-speech rights, narrowing the limits without restricting its qualities—I believe this should be done—I will not be surprised if governments in this decade and beyond fall like raindrops. Stabilization is at stake; so is cosmopolitanism. I'm fully aware, obviously, of the implications of my assessment. But the opposite, e.g. inaction is too dangerous. As a result of social media, mass culture is increasingly ungovernable.

A.V: On the other hand, sharing is closely connected with translating. In an interesting article, Varis and Blommaert argue that 'sharing' an update on Facebook is a classic case of 're-entextualization', which they describe as

> the process by means of which a piece of 'text' (a broadly defined semiotic object here) is extracted from its original context-of-use and re-inserted into an entirely different one, involving different participation frameworks, a different kind of textuality—an entire text can be condensed

into a quote, for instance—and ultimately also very different meaning outcomes. What is marginal in the source text can become important in the re-entextualized version, for instance.

(Varis and Blommaert 2015: 36)

Sharing is also a type of 're-semiotization'.

Re-semiotization, in line with the foregoing, refers to the process by means of which every 'repetition' of a sign involves an entirely new set of contextualization conditions and thus results in an entirely 'new' semiotic process, allowing new semiotic modes and resources to be involved in the repetition process.

(Varis and Blommaert 2015: 36)

They give as an example the meme 'Keep Calm and…' which has been endlessly rewritten, retranslated, combined with other memes and gone viral since the year 2000. It has even been translated into 'lolspeak' (38) in an online translation of the entire Bible. Sharing is a characteristic commonality between translation and social media. To exist, you say in your article, Ilan, a meme must travel, must be shared. The same can be said of translation. Memes transform us all in subtle ways, you assert. Again, the same goes for translation. Don't you think?

I.S: An unused meme (or else, the idea of a meme) is like a manuscript stored in a drawer, or like a tree that falls in the middle of the forest. To exist, a meme must be a bridge between at least two individuals. Needless to say, memes, within themselves, aspire to much more: dozens of recipients, hundreds, thousands, millions. The issue of connectivity starts with the act of deciphering a meme: the recipient must understand, even partially, what the sender's intended meaning is. But more is required. The ecosystem into which the meme is born is defined by irony, parody, sarcasm, mockery, ridicule and other similar cognitive tools of understanding. Unless there is a channel of shared experience between the sender and the recipient, the meme is ineffective. This frequently happens when it reaches an unintended audience, at which point it is deleted or ignored. It is important to talk about these two responses, and to ponder the way memes are also used to channel new (mis)communications in which the previously intended meaning is occasionally—and dramatically—altered.

Deliberately or otherwise, to ignore a meme is to pre-empt its message. And to delete it—which is possible only in a few platforms—is to outright cancel it. Either way, the life cycle of the meme is suddenly interrupted. When this is done, one time in a million it matters little. Yet rejecting a meme is a form of self-restraint in the receiver. 'I don't like this', the recipient might be stating; or else, 'I disagree'; or even more politically, 'I'm not ready to perpetuate this message and, therefore, I exclude myself from this community'. Clearly, receiving a meme, although seen as a passive form of behaviour, actually requires compliance and even consent.

A.V: Such concepts as 'text' or 'image' have changed in our digital age. Adding more semiotic modes to our contemporary making of meaning also implies to assemble different resources which help us to grasp today's expansion of the idea of what a text is in the era of multimodality. Indeed, language, in the case of memes, is now seen as ancillary to other semiotic modes. The different modes of intermediality appear in Web-based homepages, digital fiction, born-digital hypertext narratives, gaming, MUDs and MOOs, hyperlinked words, electronic literature, the photo-sharing application Flickr, YouTube, sites like MySpace where individuals narrate their stories on blogs, journals and discussion boards, or Facebook with its collaborative storytelling ventures, wall posts, comments and microblogging. These modes and genres are used today as new ways to tell stories where no longer are words so prominent. Graphics and animation turn the visual richness of these texts into a challenge for translators because they have altered the traditional conceptions of plot, structure, temporality, originality or agency, and at the same time demonstrated that words are only one of many semiotic systems which may be used to communicate with.

I.S: To me the meme shares qualities with the first linguistic signs recorded in caves in Cantabria in Palaeolithic times. Images are stamped on a wall to tell a story. They are anonymous. And while they are in Altamira, for instance, they bridge the local and become universal. Memes are also similar to hieroglyphics in a language that employs characters instead of letters. It goes without saying that countless memes depend on images and letters. But the base is graphic, not literal. And, as in the ancient narratives I'm invoking, they aren't static; instead, they tell stories, with a plot, no matter how incipient, how undeveloped it might be. While our technology makes us feel advanced, it draws from the same tropes humankind depends upon since the beginning of time.

A.V: The pandemic has also infected the internet, which has played a role of calming nerves during the lockdown. Memes were frequently concerned with the coronavirus. In many cases they reassured people that they were not alone. Humour, subversion and irony are mixed in all memes, and they allow users to address such a sensitive topic and express criticism of how politicians have dealt with the crisis. Some of these memes, highly topical, are difficult to understand to some elders who do not get the context. They do not have the cultural references to translate the different layers. In some countries, clever memes are used to circumvent state censorship. So, they have been used by the #BLM Movement, feminism, queer rights, climate justice and many other. However, memes can also be a weapon of harm and inflict mental and emotional damage. The coronavirus pandemic has also been an excuse to promote racism, for instance, after Trump's use of the phrase 'Chinese virus' in a tweet on 17 March 2020 (Zhu 2020). An anti-Asian sentiment was translated into images and language. This had happened in the past with other events and keeps on happening with racism in general. Sometimes these same memes are retranslated to mean the opposite. Memes spread in internet spaces and undergo multiple changes by internet users. In the case of memes related to the pandemic, they have included humour and sarcasm, but also racism, (symbolic) violence and hate. They have used negative stereotypes to expand biased attitudes against China, where it first originated. Antonio Guterres, UN Secretary General, said that migrants and refugees have been demonized as sources of the virus and denied medical treatment. He called for an 'all-out effort to end hate speech globally' amid what he called 'a tsunami of hate and xenophobia, scapegoating and scare-mongering' unleashed during the coronavirus pandemic, and added that '[a]nti-foreigner sentiment has surged online and in the streets. Anti-Semitic conspiracy theories have spread, and COVID-19-related anti-Muslim attacks have occurred' (Guterres 2020: n.p.). The so-called 'Coronavirus Karen' could also be an example here. Memes, like translations, are potentially dangerous because they are never neutral phenomena but interpretations of public dialogues.

I.S: Nothing in language is ever neutral. To engage in communication is to interpret. But memes, I agree, are semiotic hand-grenades. They are deprived of innocence; their intent is to unsettle, or, at least, to interrupt our train of thought, to disrupt it. In regard to your comment about memes circumventing censorship, censorship—I say this as a Latin American—is an engine for metaphor. Prohibition doesn't kill creativity, but forces it to redress itself.

A.V: As multimodal translations, memes subvert online official (mis)information and distort old 'normal' concepts like time, which has been the subject of endless translations that play with tense—'Next week has been exhausting!', or with the disruption of temporality—calendars represented by celebrity portraits that age decades in months, or conversely, that are presented by an identical static pose month after month after month. They also take the form of hand-washing guides with joke-lyrics that parody government slogans, or images of empty grocery shelves, panic-buying toilet paper and people wearing masks or putting on weight. But memes are more than jokes. Like translations, they help answer the question of how we all individually understand a joint experience. They are social semiotic artefacts, powerful tools for political commentary and participation, cultural translations of global issues and intersubjective experiences. As such, they serve the functions of communication and political participation. Again, like translations, they reflect the heteroglossia of perspectives.

I.S: Heteroglossia and heteronomy. Since the pandemic began, social media, obviously, has come to play an enlarged role. Twitter, Facebook, Instagram and other platforms are the channels through which people establish the parameters of their orbit. Since they are 24-hour endeavours, time as we know it vanishes. A student of mine told me the other day that this past year was 'a year without weekends'. What she meant is that she no longer perceived a difference between a working day and a day of rest: she was constantly indoor, unaware of the difference between night and day. She said that in the middle of the night, when suffering from insomnia, she would look at TikTok 'in order not to be alone'. This erasure of time might, in connection to translated memes, be approached from a different angle. After the presidential inauguration of Joe Biden on Wednesday, 20 January 2021, a meme of Senator Bernie Sanders was widely circulated online. Sanders had been photographed sitting on the inaugural platform, wearing his usual informal clothes, with mittens and a mask. It was an inspiring sight: the veteran Socialist maverick celebrating the transition of power without the regalia that goes with occasions such as this one. The photograph became an instant success among meme artists. In one meme, Sanders is sitting in Leonardo da Vinci's *The Last Supper*. In another, he is at the Yalta Conference with Churchill, Roosevelt and Stalin. And in a third one he is having lunch with workers on the steel beam in the iconic John Ebbets's photograph atop the New York City skyscraper under construction on 30 Rockefeller Plaza. The magic of these images includes the fact that Sanders—anachronistically—is painted by da Vinci around 1495, although he is an apostle next to Jesus Christ, he is in Manhattan in 1932, and he is in the Crimea on 12 February 1945. In other words, Sanders travels unimpeded through space and time in a way we, in our limited reality, cannot. That is the freedom that memes allow. They project the illusion of ubiquity, and maybe of omnipresence, which is an attribute of God.

A.V: Another thought of interest to me is the fact that the virality of GIF memes (images captioned with texts) can turn an individual's expression of hate or the sharing of stereotypical jokes into the perpetuation of bias online. As you say in your article, the young traffic with memes at an astonishing speed. This may give way to very quick and emotional responses, likes and dislikes, (politically) correct (or not) answers to sensitive topics with important consequences in the so-called 'cancel culture'.

I.S: Memes, we might say, are impulsive, unpremeditated reactions, of the kind those engaged in them don't think twice about. In that sense, they are instantaneous, automatic and, therefore, potentially inopportune. This last adjective is particularly important: to travel fast, memes need to surprise, to unsettle, to indulge in unpredictable messages. Thus, they have a somewhat disruptive quality in their nature: they maze, even startle. But, as I mentioned before, their life cycle is that of a firefly. The fact that they have a text delivered in particular languages creates a sense that we're again at the bottom of the

Tower of Babel—after the divine wrath. Tongues come and go at an astonishing speed from one end of the globe to another without much regard to nuance: it matters less what these GIF memes say than the fact that they exist. That is the phantasmagorical effect of social media: to torpedo everyone with content regardless of meaning; the objective is to stay connected, even when the reasons behind that connectivity might be unclear.

A.V: You also argue that young people see memes as democratic items.

> Through these memes, they proclaim their ideological loyalties, even when it feels as if those ideologies are hyper-sarcastic. They proclaim pop culture to be everyone's property: There is no private property, especially online; every theft is a type of appropriation.
>
> This is unusual because, in our age, the concept of appropriation is highly contested. It is ironic that the young often protest when the narrative of a disenfranchised group is stolen. Yet to create memes, they steal left and right without an ounce of shame.
>
> (Stavans 2018b: n.p.)

I feel this has to do with what Marjorie Perloff calls in another context 'unoriginal genius'. But it also makes me think of your own theory of translation and self-translation, especially when you say: 'I lived in translation without an original. In the past decade and a half, I have come to refine that view: I exist in an echo chamber of self-translated voices, all of them my own' (Stavans 2018a: 10), or when you argue that '[o]urs is a universe infused with translations' (Stavans in Sokol 2004: 84). In my opinion, this is very Borgesian: translation completes the original, broadens its meanings, opens up new interpretations, asks questions and those questions generate other questions. Translation reads the original text and discovers a journey to a rugged landscape with misty views, which is, however, worth exploring. Would you agree? Memes are translations that by sharing, by travelling, complete the original and broaden its meaning?

I.S: In memes, the concept of authenticity is revamped. Authenticity is based on copying. To be original is to exercise the dexterous talent of repurposing. Likewise, in memes the very idea of originals is pushed aside; everything is a copy, a copy of the copy and so on. One might argue, of course, that the original is the image on which the meme maker reformulates meaning; yet calling that an original is foolish since that image, by definition, is stolen. Indeed, memes make us appreciate culture as an endless sequence of thefts: to steal is to engage in conversation; to steal is to appropriate through anonymity. Perloff is not only right when she talks of 'unoriginal genius'; she actually invites us to reconsider our understanding of genius. The best memes are both genial and expressions of genius; but they aren't original. Think of Mozart, Shakespeare, Goethe and Rimbaud. We refer to them as geniuses because of the way they projected their individuality in their oeuvre. Any aspect of their work *is them*. But in memes genius is the absence of individuality; brilliance isn't confined to persons; instead, it is the result of group efforts. Memes aren't expressions of personal quality, nor are they representations of intellectual property. Memes are masks behind which pluralities hide.

A.V: Another seminal characteristic of memes is their multimodality. In this sense, I think they are a very good example of the new concept of 'text' in our visual culture. Communication today implies an inevitable combination of different media. Scholars are moving from a language-centred model of a decade ago to another one which underlines the interconnection among media. Words, images, colours, sounds, bodies, gestures, tastes, spaces, movements, cities, architecture, all communicate and make clear that no single disciplinary framework can be an adequate approach to our multimodal world. If we want to understand how meaning is produced, expanding the idea of language seems inevitable.

The stories told through memes show that non-traditional texts need to be translated in new ways. Given this state of affairs, expanding the field of translation studies seems to be an urgent goal. Within this new semiotic landscape, translation needs to broaden its scope. Developments in multimodal studies in the field of translation have already begun to change our idea of what translation is. In fact, many scholars claim that in our global and visual culture the question of what constitutes a translation is under radical review. Arduini and Nergaard (2011) urge for a different way of facing the great epistemological questions of what we know and how we know. This is echoed by Gentzler (2017) who underlines the need to translate without borders, to understand translation as an ongoing process of movement, manoeuvring, traversing boundaries, changing and adapting. He argues that rather than thinking about translation as a somewhat secondary process of ferrying ideas across borders, we think beyond borders to culture as a whole, reconceiving of translation as an always primary, primordial and proactive process that continually introduces new ideas, forms or expressions and pathways for change into cultures. Memes are translated communications, one of the best examples of the new concept of 'text' in our multimodal culture and, furthermore, an excellent exemplification of the 'outward turn' in translation studies. The multimodal nature of memes makes us aware of how urgent it is for translation studies to turn *outwards*, to use Susan Bassnett's term. This means translation studies needs to engage more with other disciplines so that it will not become introspective, as we fear has been happening, with scholars talking only to one another within the field. In a dialogue with Anthony Pym, Bassnett describes translation in a way that could be applied to memes: 'Promoting translation [is] a creative act, one which always involves language and is also political [...] We learn what cannot be said' (Bassnett 2017: 150).

I.S: The old definitions of translation have become obsolete. By this I mean that translation, as I've said before, is much more than simply conveying a text in a language other than the one that originally houses it. For me translation is a way of life. I'm an immigrant. Switching languages is a daily affair. I negotiate who I am all the time by using different codes depending on the social environment I find myself in. Translation, in my eyes, isn't static; it is like jazz—amorphous, nervous, improvisational. To be frank, I have little interest in translation studies as a discipline because it confines what is existential to me to a narrow academic field. Translation is a strategy of survival; it is the tool through which I become a different person depending on the circumstance.

A.V: Memes are internet translations. They are examples of multimodal, multi-authorial and multi-layered new texts that do not have a single interpretation and, as Maitland asserts, they are hermeneutic reflections that arise 'from the co-presence of a literal signification suggestive of a secondary meaning that can only be understood by a detour through the meaning of the first' (Maitland 2017: 38). They are palimpsests, text upon image, image upon image, sound upon sound, all full of parody, humour, hate, ostracism and always, interpretation upon interpretation. That is why Maitland argues in her lecture that:

> The cultural stimulus that is copied in the meme functions as the 'source text' of translation. This source text is interpreted, imitated, parodied, transformed, reshaped, and 'translated' by Internet users, turning it into something new, a 'third object', alike and akin to the original cultural stimulus, yet undeniably different. Just like a translation, this new form is intended to find a new audience in a new time and new place.
>
> (Maitland 2019: n.p.)

In some books, you describe yourself not as an original but as a second original (Stavans 2020b: 14) who feels attracted by masks (Stavans and Villoro 2014: 147–148). You have also said that you like anthologies because they give the reader multiple points of view and in your book on 'cellfies' you argue that 'our self isn't a unity but a multiplicity' (Stavans 2017: 7). What similarities do you find between selfies and memes?

I.S.:   Selfies are palimpsests, too; they are curated, instant, ephemeral versions of the self. Like memes, they exist by creating a community of those who are included—the sender of the selfie chooses its recipients—and also those who are excluded. The difference between 'selfie' and 'cellfie', and even between these two spellings and a third one, 'selfy', is essential: one highlights the self, another the cell phone and the third the monetary transaction engaged by the photograph that is being shared. To me selfies are marketable versions of who we are; they reduce us to a convenient profile, the equivalent of a meme. In fact, selfies (notice my choice of spelling) are often intervened by the sender or someone else, de facto becoming memes. That intervention might be a way of beautifying the picture; or it might be an aggression, a way of demeaning it. In any case, they are similar to translation in that they refashion a real object in subjective ways, thus modifying its meaning. You could call this 'de-meaning', since by changing the meaning, the meme causes a loss which might involve respect. The translation gives a different kind of respect to the original.

A. V: The coronavirus has endorsed new meanings to such words as touching, distance, fear, isolation, strangeness and disorientation. In sum, this small virus has had the enormous capacity to rewrite life and death. The virus is our most powerful rewriter today, a translator who is obliging us to reread concepts, even ways of life. It took us by surprise, although this is not new. Similar disasters, taking the form of 'earthquakes, deluges, famines, plagues of insects [...] are recurrent visitors in the theater of human affairs' (Stavans 2020a: xiii). The title of your anthology, *And We Came Outside and Saw the Stars Again*, was inspired by the last line of Dante's *Inferno*, in which the poet and Virgil emerge from their journey through hell to once again view the beauty of the heavens. But this time we have new ways of representing fear, isolation and loss; we have new forms of translating the virus's translations back. In the story written for *And We Came Outside and Saw the Stars Again*, Juan Villoro argues that memes, GIFs, poems, songs, art, concerts, dreams or listening to the dreams of others, represent forms of imagination which are helping us in this crisis. While governments are cutting funds in the cultural sector, the irony is that we are surviving thanks to the arts. Villoro mentions Churchill's claim that Britain won the war because they decided not to close theatres. 'The species persists through forms of representation of reality' (Villoro in Stavans 2020a: 225–226). Memes are one of these forms of representing and translating reality. By rewriting and translating what is happening, memes and other digital platforms have revealed many things of our own selves and been a selfie/cellfie of contemporary society. As Carlos Fonseca argues in the story he writes for your anthology,

> [t]he paradox behind this pandemic is that it has made evident the world in which we were already living: a world of isolation, of frontiers and walls, a world where the elderly are secluded and forgotten, a xenophobic world, where death is something invisible that happens always behind closed doors and against which we prove incapable of mourning. A world that mixes the possibilities of technological globalization—Zoom, Skype, FaceTime— with the tightening of borders and the rise of contemporary nationalisms [...] Sometimes I feel that the logic of the virus, which is that of repetition and difference, is precisely the logic of rumor and of the media. Tweet and retweet.

The logic of post-truth. Perhaps the uncanny sense of unreality that pervades this crisis comes from the fact that now, more than ever, we are living through a catastrophe that is experienced online.

(Fonseca in Stavans 2020a: 326)

I.S: Memes are astonishingly creative forms of communication. Insofar as social media remains uninterrupted, they are the go-to form of informal encounter, taking people out of their Robinson Crusoe Island into a marketplace of meaning. Like guns, they aren't dangerous onto themselves; it is who uses them that gives them an edge. The pandemic is the most sobering event of our lifetime. It is a calamity of the magnitude of the bubonic plague in the Middle Ages, the Napoleonic Wars, the First and Second World Wars and similar transformative moments in human history. The fact that we have moved into Zoom in order to continue our life and that memes have become transactional capsules, is evidence of human adaptability. As Plato suggests in *The Republic*, 'our need will be the real creator'. One might take this to mean, in the popular imagination, that 'necessity is the mother of creation'. I find memes extraordinary in their resourcefulness. Can we one day create with them a narrative that is the equivalent of a novel, one capable of moving us inside? Maybe. The language of memes is an infinite translation.

References

Arduini, S., and Nergaard, S. (2011). 'Translation: A new paradigm', *Translation. A Transdisciplinary Journal*, 1(1), 8–17.

Bassnett, S. (2017). 'On the direction of Translation Studies: Susan Bassnett and Anthony Pym in dialogue', *Cultus: The Journal of Intercultural Mediation and Communication* 10(1): 145–152.

Chesterman, A. (2016). *Memes of Translation*, Amsterdam and Philadelphia: John Benjamins.

Cho, S.-E., and Suh, J. (2021). 'Translating Korean beauty YouTube channels for a global audience', in R. Desjardins, C. Larsonneur, and P. Lacour (Eds.), *When Translation Goes Digital: Case Studies and Critical Reflections*, London: Palgrave Macmillan, 173–197.

Gentzler, E. (2015). 'Translation without borders', *Translation* 4: 1–15.

Gentzler, E. (2017). *Translation and Rewriting in the Age of Post-Translation Studies*, Abingdon and New York: Routledge.

Guterres, A. (2020). 'Appeal to address and counter COVID-19 hate speech' (8 May, 2020), https://www.un.org/sg/en/content/sg/speeches/2020-05-08/appeal-address-and-counter-covid-19-hate-speech.

John, N. (2016). *The Age of Sharing*, Cambridge: Polity Press.

Lee, T. K. (2021). 'Distribution and translation', *Applied Linguistic Review*, (ahead of print), 000010151520200139. https://doi.org/10.1515/applirev-2020-0139

Lee, T. K., and Chan, S. W.-K. (2018). 'Transcreating memes: Chinese concrete poetry', in J. Boase-Beier, L. Fisher, and H. Furukawa (Eds.), *The Palgrave Handbook of Literary Translation*, London: Palgrave Macmillan, 187–206.

Maitland, S. (2017). *What Is Cultural Translation?*, London and New York: Bloomsbury Academic.

Maitland, S. (2019). 'What can memes teach us about cultural translation?', Lecture at the University of Edinburgh (16 October, 2019), https://www.iash.ed.ac.uk/event/sarah-maitland-goldsmiths-university-london-what-can-memes-teach-us-about-cultural-translation.

Otsuji, E., and Pennycook, A. (2021). 'Interartefactual translation: Metrolingualism and resemiotization', in T. K. Lee (Ed.), *The Routledge Handbook of Translation and the City*, Abingdon and New York: Routledge, 59–76.

Sokol, N. (2004). *Ilan Stavans: Eight Conversations*, Madison, WI: The University of Wisconsin Press.

Stavans, I. (2017). *I Love My Selfie*, Durham, NC and London: Duke University Press.

Stavans, I. (2018a). *On Self-Translation: Meditations on Language*, Albany, NY: State University of New York Press.

Stavans, I. (2018b). 'Friday takeaway: Memetics', *Daily Hampshire Gazett* (8/9/2018), https://www.gazettenet.com/friday-takeaway-19324875.

Stavans, I. (Ed.). (2020a). *And We Came Outside and Saw the Stars Again*, New York: Restless Books.

Stavans, I. (2020b). 'Self-Translation como survival mecanismo', *Ínsula* septiembre, 885, 13–15.

Stavans, I., and Villoro, J. (2014). *El ojo en la nuca*, Barcelona: Anagrama.

Varis, P., and Blommaert, J. (2015). 'Conviviality and collectives on social media: Virality, memes, and new social structures', *Multilingual Margins* 2(1): 31–45.

Zhu, H. (2020). 'Countering COVID-19-related anti-Chinese racism with translanguaged swearing on social media', *Multilingua* 39(5): 607–616.

Index

Page numbers followed by "n" indicate note.

Printed and bound by CPI Group (UK) Ltd, Croydon, CR0 4YY

11/04/2025

01844010-0008